Keep It Simple

DAVE O'DONNELL

Publisher by MCC Publishing

ISBN 978-1-0687812-0-9 (Print)
ISBN 978-1-0687812-3-0 (Ebook)

To My Family.

Table of Contents

INTRODUCTION

We often hear the saying "Keep It Simple" bandied about in various contexts in life. Reduce stress in your life by keeping it simple, get a better sense of clarity by keeping it simple, increase productivity and efficiency by keeping it simple and so on and so forth. There is common sense in this approach, usually when we "Keep It Simple," we see positive results. However, this is particularly important when it comes to the journey of recovering from alcoholism or addiction. If you're reading this, you will understand the complex process of overcoming addiction, the path to recovery. You might wonder, "How can something as complex as addiction recovery be simplified?" Well, that's precisely what this book aims to explore.

In Alcoholics Anonymous (AA) and other 12-step programs, the principle of "Keep It Simple" isn't just a catchy phrase, it serves as a lifeline. During my own recovery journey, I often got caught up in overthinking, second-guessing, and convoluted strategies to maintain sobriety. The constant mental chatter would overwhelm me. However, when I started embracing the "Keep It Simple" principle, I discovered a clearer, more attainable route to recovery. This straightforward mantra not only helped me stay sober but also transformed my approach to life, relationships, and personal growth.

The power of simplicity in the recovery journey cannot be overstated. Overcoming addiction is fraught with emotional, psychological, physical, and social challenges. In the midst of this chaos, simplicity acts as a lens, bringing clarity and helping us focus on what truly matters—our commitment to sobriety and well-being. Amid temptations, emotional turmoil, and complicated relationships, a simplified approach serves as a steadying force, guiding us through the storm.

As I write these words, an old saying comes to mind: "It's a long road that has no bends." I am traveling that road, and it has led me here to a place of clarity, reflection, and gratitude. My journey has brought me to a profound acceptance: I acknowledged that my life had become unmanageable, and I accepted what I am, a recovering alcoholic and addict who once walked the treacherous path of addiction but has now found the path of recovery. Thanks to the unwavering support and love of my family, the wisdom of Alcoholics Anonymous (AA), and the guiding light of the "Keep It Simple" principle, I have discovered a way of life that is both fulfilling and beautifully simple.

There was a time when my life was anything but simple a chaotic dance with alcohol and drugs that grew more entangled with each passing day. I was trapped in a web of lies, excuses, and the exhausting effort to maintain a facade of normalcy, which I had perfected. I was deceitful, delusional, and deeply troubled. The complexities of my addiction led me to dark places physically, mentally, and emotionally. But like many others who reach their breaking point, I encountered a moment of reckoning my Rock Bottom. This was my game changer; the moment I realized I no longer wanted the life I was living. I longed for freedom, to become the person I was meant to be. I made a choice that transformed me, a choice to pursue a life of fulfilment and purpose. And so, I found myself stepping into the rooms of AA, surrounded by others who shared their stories of struggle, triumph, and the pursuit of sobriety. In these rooms, I discovered the strength of simplicity and the profound peace it brings. The first few years were tough, okay I was not drinking and drugging, but my head was all over the place. These early years were also tough on my family. Yes, they were happy that I was committed to keeping sober, but they also experienced my moods and struggles as I tried to deal with the waves of emotion that would wash over me daily. All the emotion I had suppressed for a long time whilst I was in active addiction. I had not developed emotionally as I should have, and now it was happening all at once, it was scary and confusing at times. I hadn't developed the skills to deal with it all properly. I enrolled in a course which opened me up to emotions, how many there are, what triggers them and how best to respond to them. It was a great experience, and I learned a lot about myself and my compulsion for control but still I knew there was something else that I needed, something else that was the key to me experiencing peace of mind.

It was in AA, that I encountered a simple phrase that would change the course of my recovery journey forever—the "Keep It Simple" principle. These three words might seem unassuming, even oversimplified. I had seen this framed on walls in the rooms and listened to members using it when they shared, but in the early years it didn't click with me. I wasn't able to grasp this remarkably simple yet powerful principle. Just like it says in the AA Big Book somethings quickly sometimes slowly, I kept finding myself coming back to it whenever I struggled (which was most of the time). At first it was like there was something deep inside of me guiding me back to it. Then this draw grew stronger pulling me like an invisible magnet regardless of how I felt, "Keep it Simple, Keep it Simple." There was a voice a sensation inside of me telling me that if I surrendered to it, the realisation would come to me. So I surrendered and it did. As I embraced this principle, I began to realise the wisdom these three words held. The "Keep It Simple" principle became my compass, guiding me through the maze of emotions, challenges, and uncertainties. It wasn't about providing a quick fix or a one-size-fits-all solution. It was about returning to basics, finding clarity amidst confusion, and reclaiming a sense of self that was obscured by the haze of addiction.

This principle, which had initially seemed like a just a saying, gradually transformed into a way of life. And is still transforming me as I write. It wasn't about simplifying my approach to recovery; it was about simplifying my approach to life itself. It led me to question the unnecessary complications I had allowed to seep into every corner of my existence. The "Keep it Simple" principle introduced me to the concept of keeping my life small. So let me explain this please. I didn't retreat from the world like some kind of a hermit, I did the opposite, I went out to embrace the world in a mindful and intentional way. I began to develop a selective sense of who and what is really important to me, what do I need and how can I live my life the best I can. This was the beginning of progress which I believe will continue for the rest of my life.

In the pages that follow, I invite you to come along on this journey with me. A journey through my eyes, I have lived in the darkness of addiction, and I have found peace and strength within my family, the rooms of AA, and woven the "Keep It Simple" principle into the fabric of my recovery. This book isn't just a collection of ideas—it's a reflection of my individual experiences, a testimony to the transformative power of simplicity.

From breaking common fears that complicate recovery, to embracing the basics of a twelve step program, and extending simplicity into other aspects of life. Its applicable to relationships and personal growth and how we examine ourselves, our mind, body and soul in an integrated way. I do not hold myself out there as an expert, far from it, I am learning every day and making mistakes every day. The object of this book is to serve as a guide. I want to share my experience to help others – it's that simple. Whether you're taking the first step into recovery or you're far along in your journey, the pages that follow I hope will help you to strip away the drama and unnecessary complexities and focus on the essentials.

We all want a life beyond our wildest dreams—a life of freedom, purpose, and meaningful connections. This life is within our grasp, and the key to reaching it is simpler than you might think. As you read these words, know that you're not alone. If you are facing challenges with addiction, searching for clarity, or looking for a path ahead, my hope is this book can offer you some guidance and support. The "Keep It Simple" principle is a reminder that amidst the chaos, there is a path to peace. I know how difficult it can be to focus when we come into recovery at first. Bearing this in mind I have set out to keep this book simple and concise, to strip it back as best I can so that it is clear and easy to digest. In the main I have used an inclusive language writing style using "we" instead of "you" and "I." I have done this purposely in order to attempt to better connect with you the readers, my hope is that it will create a sense of unity and shared experience, something you will be able to identify with. So, let's journey together, one page at a time, as we explore the richness, depth and beautifully simple joys that come with recovery and sobriety.

THE ESSENCE OF SIMPLICITY IN RECOVERY

Recovery might seem complicated at first, and it's understandable to think so. After all, we're addressing something that has upended our lives and the lives of those close to us. But the truth is, the heart of recovery is surprisingly simple. So, let's break it down.

When Alcoholics Anonymous began, its founders, Dr. Bob Smith and Bill Wilson, knew they were facing a complex challenge: addiction. Life with addiction is a mess. You've got cravings, emotional rollercoasters, and all kinds of thoughts spinning around in your head, that Stinkin Thinkin can bring you to some crazy places. But Dr. Bob and Bill Wilson made a vital choice—they chose to keep the core of recovery simple. Now, why is that? Because when we're caught up in the storm of addiction, simple is good. Simple is a lifebuoy that keeps us afloat. Dr. Bob used to say, "Let's not mess this up; let's "Keep It Simple." And that simple advice could very well be why so many people find their way back to a stable life through AA.

At the core of recovery is simplicity. Personally, this meant stripping away complications and returning to the basics. The basics are your best friend. And the basics are simple: stay sober one day at a time, be honest with yourself and others, lean on your family and community for support, and keep improving yourself. So let's dive into the basic elements that make up the essence of simplicity in recovery.

A DAY AT A TIME.

In the journey of recovery, we embrace the philosophy of taking sobriety one day at a time. This simple yet powerful approach allows us to greet each new day with a focused intention, rather than getting overwhelmed by the daunting prospect of lifelong sobriety. Every morning presents a fresh opportunity, a blank slate where the only commitment we make is to stay sober for just that day. This method effectively breaks down the monumental task of recovery into daily, achievable goals, making the path forward seem less intimidating and more manageable. Each day, as we awaken, we are faced with a choice—an essential, deliberate decision on whether to continue our commitment to sobriety. It's a question that, despite its simplicity, holds profound implications for our journey. By choosing sobriety each day, we build a sequence of successful, sober days that gradually weave into the fabric of a healthier lifestyle. This day-by-day approach doesn't just simplify recovery; it empowers us, giving us the confidence and resilience to say "yes" to sobriety with each new dawn. In keeping our focus narrow and our goals straightforward, we find the strength to continue, and each "yes" reinforces our resolve, keeping us anchored on the path to healing.

BE HONEST.

Honesty stands as one of the most formidable challenges in recovery, largely because addiction is so often a disease of deceit. We've constructed elaborate falsehoods, lying to ourselves and to those around us to protect or to perpetuate our habits. But at the heart of any true recovery, honesty must prevail. It begins with the foundational acknowledgment of our struggles—that we are indeed grappling with a problem and that we require assistance to overcome it. Honesty extends beyond this admission; it involves a continual practice of recognizing our mistakes, owning our missteps, and making earnest efforts to rectify them.

Embracing honesty in recovery can be daunting and at times, deeply uncomfortable, particularly as we confront the realities we may have long avoided or obscured with substances. Yet, this pursuit of truth is liberating. Honesty acts like a beam of light cutting through dense fog, clarifying our vision and illuminating our path forward. It allows us to see ourselves and our situations with newfound clarity and, often, a renewed sense of purpose. By choosing to be honest, we not only cleanse our lives of the toxins of deception, but we also open doors to deeper, more meaningful connections with others. In recovery, each moment of truth strengthens our commitment to this new way of living, reinforcing our resolve and helping us navigate the complexities of healing with integrity and grace.

FAMILY AND COMMUNITY.

I am fortunate to have a loving family and close friends who support me in my recovery. I know I am blessed as this is not the case for everyone on the recovery journey. But, if like me, you are lucky to have a family and friends around you when you are getting better and trying to stay clean and sober then you will know how important they are. They are the ones who love us no matter what and they provide a shoulder to cry on. Of course, not all families are helpful, but when they are it's like having a home team cheering us on. All they want is the best for us. They may not get everything we're going through, but their love makes the hard stuff that bit easier.

Community, these are the people who actually know what we're dealing with because they've been through it too. Imagine walking into a room and not having to explain why you feel a certain way; people just get it. This community is where we can talk freely, pick up useful tips, and even offer advice to others. Feeling like we belong somewhere makes everything easier, especially when we're trying to quit something that used to be a big part of our life. Family makes us feel like we belong because, well, they are family. Community makes us feel like we belong because everyone's fighting the same battle. AA or any other twelve step fellowship is there for one simple reason—to support each other. When we're down, struggling with cravings, or when we're just having a terrible day, that community is there to pick us up. And when things are going well, we're there to support others. It's a give-and-take relationship, simple but powerful.

Family and community provide a watchful and caring eye. They will notice any changes if we're slipping back into old behaviours before we notice ourself. They are a powerful and effective early warning system that will keep us on track. Simple and effective. Family and community work together like a tag team. Our family gives us that emotional boost, the love that everyone needs. Our community gives us practical advice, the benefit of experience, understanding strength and hope. When we have both in our corner, we're setting ourself up for a win. Family and community helps bolster us against the potholes and blind bends on the road that leads to the simple heart of recovery, Love and Support.

BE PRESENT.

Living in the moment is not just a practice—it's a vital part of recovery. In the early stages of sobriety, I found myself frequently caught up in the whirlwind of future uncertainties. My anxiety would skyrocket, creating turmoil not just for me, but also for my family. Learning to embrace simplicity helped ground me in the present. I realized that all I needed to focus on was making good choices today, each day, one step at a time. This doesn't mean abandoning future planning altogether. Planning is essential, and having goals gives direction and purpose to our lives. However, the key is to plan without becoming attached to specific outcomes. This attachment often leads to disappointment, frustration, and resentment when things inevitably don't go as precisely as we hoped.

Understanding that there is no such thing as a perfect plan is crucial because perfection is an impossible standard. We are all human and inherently imperfect. When we encounter setbacks, it's important to see them not as catastrophes that derail our entire plan, but as minor bumps in the road—part and parcel of life's journey. Adopting a straightforward approach allows us to adapt and move forward without getting bogged down by the intricacies of our expectations. This simplicity in our mindset can significantly alleviate the stress of needing to control every detail and helps us to stay focused on our recovery. By being present, we allow ourselves the flexibility to respond to life as it happens, making adjustments and continuing on our path with resilience and grace.

LET IT GO.

Active addiction breeds an obsession with control, an irony that never escapes me. In the midst of addiction, our lives spiral into chaos and drama, yet paradoxically, we often believe we have everything under control. We overthink and build complex stories, layer upon layer, deluding ourselves into believing that we are masterfully orchestrating our lives. However, the philosophy of "Keep It Simple" teaches a different lesson—it encourages us to let go, to surrender our illusion of control to something greater than ourselves. Whether it's a higher power, the universal energy, or the natural synchronicity that weaves through our existence, trusting in these forces allows us to operate in harmony with the world around us. Embracing life on its own terms, without the constant need to manipulate every outcome, brings a profound sense of peace and alignment.

This shift in focus has been transformative for my recovery and overall well-being. Most days, I now wake up viewing each morning as a clean slate, a precious opportunity to maintain sobriety, to grow as a person, and to appreciate the simple joys of life. This new perspective has been instrumental in building a sustainable recovery. It helped me to not just count days of sobriety but to make the days count, accumulating into weeks, months, and eventually years of living clean and sober. By simplifying my approach and recalibrating my expectations, I've found a way to live more fully, embracing each moment as it comes with gratitude and resilience. This approach doesn't just manage addiction; it enhances every aspect of life, making each day a fresh start and a chance for renewal.

SELF-IMPROVEMENT.

Recovery is more than just breaking free from addiction; it's a journey towards becoming a better person and discovering our purpose. This transformation doesn't have to be complex. In fact, becoming a better person and finding our purpose can be achieved through simple, positive changes in our daily lives. Whether it's picking up a good book, engaging in regular exercise, or nurturing a mindset open to growth and learning—every small action counts. Over time, these small steps accumulate, leading to substantial change. So, what does "Keep It Simple" mean in the context of self-improvement? It means focusing on one thing at a time, rather than overwhelming ourselves with an exhaustive list of everything we want to change. Consider the analogy of eating an elephant—one bite at a time. For example, if you aim to improve your health, start with a manageable goal rather than an ambitious overhaul. Instead of immediately cutting out all sugar, exercising daily, and overhauling your sleep schedule, begin with something straightforward, like a ten-minute daily walk. Frame this goal positively: "A daily ten-minute walk enhances both my physical and mental health, exposes me to fresh air, and helps me appreciate the world around me, making me feel good." This positive framing not only makes the goal less intimidating but also more compelling because our minds are drawn to goals that are perceived as pleasurable.

By keeping it simple, we are more likely to stick with them. It's easy to get fired up about big grandiose goals, but it's just as easy to burn out fast if we're trying to do too much. Self-improvement doesn't have to be complicated to be effective. A simple approach to self-improvement doesn't just make us better at any particular thing -it makes us better at life.

HOW SIMPLICITY SERVES AS THE CORNERSTONE OF RECOVERY

When we're battling addiction, our mind is often cluttered with worry, guilt, and complicated plans for how to either hide the addiction or quit it altogether. By aiming to simplify our life and our approach, we're clearing away the mental debris that prevents us from focusing on what's profoundly important: getting sober and staying that way. Don't make things harder than they have to be. This is like building a house, we have to lay strong foundation before we put up the walls and the roof. "Keep It Simple" is our foundation. Once that's stable, we can then start adding other things like mending relationships, figuring out our career or what is our purpose.

The idea of "Keep It Simple" starts with our daily routine. In the early stages of recovery, it's crucial to establish a simple, structured day-to-day life. Wake up at the same time, eat regular meals, attend meetings, go to bed at a reasonable hour. This may sound trivial, but remember, we're building a foundation, and every brick counts. The predictability can be comforting and can help avoid the chaos that often accompanies addiction. The basic structure also provides fewer opportunities for triggers that might tempt us to go back to old habits. The basic structure helps us from getting overwhelmed, because when we are overwhelmed staying clean and sober becomes a lot harder.

A big part of recovery is dealing with emotions and past mistakes. This can make anyone's head spin. But again, simplicity is our friend here. We don't have to sort out all your emotional baggage at once. We'll have time for that. Right now, our job is to not pick up a drink or use drugs, no matter what we're feeling. We'll learn more coping skills as we go along, but until then, stick with what works, even if it's as simple as taking deep breaths or counting to ten.

Simple doesn't mean easy. Staying sober is hard work, so making it more complicated than it has to be won't help. Life's going to throw curveballs our way; that's guaranteed. We might lose our job, or a relationship might end. But even in those hard times, the simple goal remains the same: stay sober. Focus on the main mission, don't pick up no matter what. It's our cornerstone, the thing we come back to when everything else is up in the air. No matter what's happening around us, our number one job is to protect our sobriety.

"Keep It Simple" also applies to our emotional well-being. It's easy to get caught up in regrets about the past or fears about the future. But these thoughts, while natural, don't serve our ultimate goal of sobriety. Instead, try to focus on the present. How are we feeling right now? What can we do today to strengthen our sobriety? By narrowing our attention to what's immediately in front of us we can reduce the emotional clutter that can distract us from our goal. "Keep It Simple" just for today!

It's also worth mentioning that simplicity extends to our interpersonal relationships. During your time of active addiction, relationships might have been complicated, marked by dishonesty or manipulation. We are presented with the opportunity to simplify these interactions. Be honest about our struggles and our boundaries. Make it clear that our recovery is our priority and develop relationships that support that goal.

In summary, simplicity in recovery means clearing away the noise and distractions to focus on what truly matters: building a sober, fulfilling life. Every decision we make, every relationship we maintain, every step we take in our recovery journey should align with this straightforward but incredibly potent objective. So, when we feel overwhelmed, remember the wise words of

Dr. Bob: "Let's Keep It Simple." Simple is all we need. And Simple is exactly what saves us.

CHAPTER ONE SUMMARY

Simplicity:

Serves as a lifebuoy in the chaotic sea of addiction, making it easier to focus on sobriety.

A Day At A Time:

The basics of recovery are staying sober one day at a time, being honest with ourselves and others, relying on family and community for support, and focusing on self-improvement.

Sobriety:

Focus on being sober just for today, breaking down the larger task into manageable chunks.

Honesty:

Essential in facing our addiction and making meaningful progress in recovery.

Family and Community:

Both serve as essential pillars of support, with family offering emotional support and community providing practical advice and mutual understanding.

Living in the Moment:

The "Keep It Simple" philosophy teaches us to focus on the present and make good choices today, rather than getting overwhelmed by the future.

Self-Improvement:

Simplify self-improvement goals, focusing on one thing at a time to make them achievable.

Daily Routine:

A simple, structured routine helps build a foundation for recovery and minimizes triggers and opportunities for relapse.

Emotional Well-Being:

Focusing on the present moment simplifies emotional management, reducing distractions from our sobriety goal.

Interpersonal Relationships:

Simplify by being honest and making recovery a priority.

Main Points of Chapter One:

The objective is to clear away distractions and complications, enabling full focus on building a sober, fulfilling life. The mantra *"Let's Keep it Simple,"* as advocated by Dr. Bob, remains the cornerstone of effective recovery.

CHAPTER 2

BREAKING DOWN COMPLEXITY

The world thrives on complexity, from the challenges of daily life to the intricate patterns of our emotions. At times, this complexity feels overwhelming, making recovery seem daunting. It's easy to get lost in myths and fears, such as the cliché "Once an Addict, Always an Addict." This phrase paints a bleak picture, implying a never-ending struggle, as if addiction defines us forever. But no one chooses to become addicted. We got caught up trying to escape something we couldn't handle. Recovery, however, offers us a chance to learn the skills we need to face discomfort. The journey may be long and winding, but with each step, we move closer to understanding, self-acceptance, and a fulfilling life.

Let's simplify recovery. Below are seven common myths we encounter on this journey. While recovery might initially seem daunting, full of uncertainty and change, these myths create a mental fog around the truth. Recovery is often perceived as a path filled with hurdles and endless battles. But what if we shift our perspective? By dispelling myths and addressing fears with knowledge, we can uncover the clarity and simplicity recovery truly offers. My own head was filled with myths when I started out first. I am no different to anyone else embarking on this journey. I sought out advice and counsel from those who have travelled before me.

The advice they gave me in addition to tips and coping mechanisms helped me to deal with the myths. I have set out below my experience and the advice I was given so that I may help you the reader as you journey through this stage.

MYTH 1: "RECOVERY MEANS I NEED TO BE PERFECT."

Reality:

Recovery is about progress, not perfection. It's about trying, learning from mistakes, and moving forward. Striving for perfection is like chasing the wind—you'll exhaust yourself without ever catching it. Imagine running a never-ending race; eventually, you'll wear yourself out and feel isolated.

However, when we accept our imperfections, life becomes simpler and more enjoyable. We become relatable, and people feel more comfortable around us. This honesty builds stronger connections and invites support when we need it most. Embracing imperfection turns a rocky path into a smoother trail, where friends walk alongside us, making the journey less lonely and more meaningful.

Actionable Step:

Set small, achievable goals. Instead of aiming for perfection, focus on consistent progress. Celebrate each step forward, no matter how small.

Practical Advice:

Keep a journal where you reflect on your daily progress. Write down what you've learned from any mistakes, and how you plan to grow from them. This will help you see that recovery is a journey, not a destination.

MYTH 2: "I'VE FAILED BEFORE, SO WHY BOTHER?"

Reality:

Setbacks don't mean failure; they're opportunities to learn and grow. Think of recovery like learning to ride a bike—you might fall a few times before finding your balance. Each fall teaches you something new, helping you build resilience, which is like a mental muscle for tackling challenges. Every morning offers a fresh start, a blank page to write a new chapter in your story. Don't let past stumbles define today. Recovery is a journey where every step, no matter how small, is progress. The bumps along the way highlight your strength and determination, making your success even more meaningful.

Actionable Step:

Reframe setbacks as learning experiences. When you stumble, take a moment to reflect on what triggered it and how you can approach similar situations differently in the future.

Practical Advice:

Start each day with a fresh mindset. Remind yourself that every new day is a chance to rewrite your story. Consider using affirmations or motivational quotes to keep your focus on the progress you're making.

MYTH 3: "RECOVERY IS JUST ABOUT QUITTING."

Reality:

Recovery isn't just about quitting a harmful behaviour; it's about cultivating personal growth and wellness in every aspect of life—physical health, emotional well-being, relationships, career, and spirituality. It's like tending to a garden: removing the weeds (addiction) is just the first step. Recovery is about planting and nurturing new, healthy habits that allows us to thrive.

This journey of transformation is ongoing. Each day brings new challenges, joys, and milestones, helping you grow into the person you were meant to be. Recovery isn't just about survival; it's about living a life filled with purpose and meaning.

Actionable Step:

Engage in activities that promote holistic well-being, such as regular exercise, meditation, or pursuing hobbies. These activities help rebuild your life beyond just quitting a harmful behavior.

Practical Advice:

Create a "self-care" wheel that includes all areas of your life physical, psychological, emotional, spiritual. personal, professional Regularly assess where you are and identify areas that need more attention or improvement. This helps ensure that your recovery is well-rounded and fulfilling. See example of self-care wheel below. Use whatever headings you feel are applicable to where you are now in life for your self-care wheel.

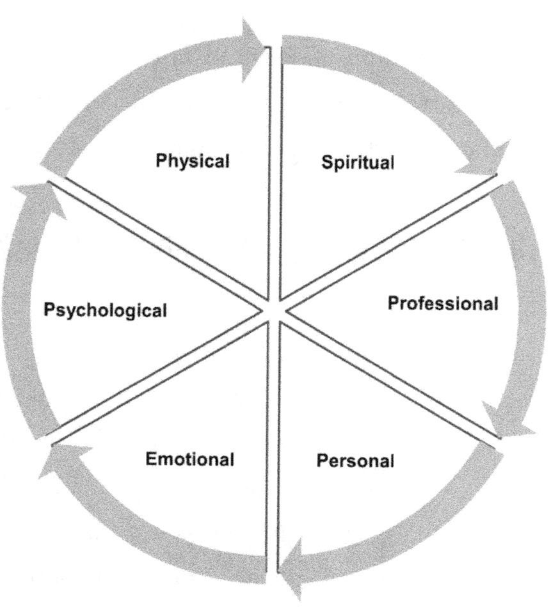

For guidance purposes I have listed some items under the various headings in the Self Care Wheel below.

Personal:	Professional:
<ul><li>Reflect on who you are and what makes you special.</li><li>Plan and set goals.</li><li>Be available for friends and spend time with family.</li><li>Learn a new skill.</li></ul>	<ul><li>Set boundaries.</li><li>Use your vacation time.</li><li>Learn to say no.</li><li>Leave work at work.</li></ul>
Emotional:	**Psychological:**
<ul><li>Laugh.</li><li>Practice self-love.</li><li>Cry.</li><li>Community Engagement.</li></ul>	<ul><li>Join a support group.</li><li>Take time for self-reflection.</li><li>Therapy of counselling.</li><li>Keep a journal.</li></ul>
Physical:	**Spiritual:**
<ul><li>Exercise.</li><li>Eat healthy.</li><li>Regular sleep.</li><li>Hugs and holding hands</li></ul>	<ul><li>Practice forgiveness.</li><li>Spend time in nature.</li><li>Volunteer to help others.</li><li>Sing or dance.</li></ul>

MYTH 4: "I CAN'T MANAGE LIFE WITHOUT MY SUBSTANCE OF CHOICE."

Reality:

Facing life without substances may seem scary, but it's like learning to ride a bike—it gets easier with practice. In early recovery, you might feel wobbly and vulnerable, but over time, you'll develop the emotional skills needed to navigate life's challenges. Recovery allows you to feel emotions deeply, both the highs and the lows, helping you understand yourself better.

Embracing your emotions without numbing them builds emotional strength, much like lifting weights strengthens muscles. As you grow stronger, you'll discover what truly brings you happiness and fulfilment, making the journey through life more meaningful.

Actionable Step:

Develop emotional coping strategies, such as mindfulness, breathing exercises, or talking to a trusted friend or therapist. These strategies help you face challenges without turning to substances.

Practical Advice:

Create a daily practice of checking in with yourself. Ask, "What am I feeling right now?" and "How can I address these feelings in a healthy way?" Over time, this self-awareness becomes a powerful tool in managing life without relying on substances.

MYTH 5: "I'LL BE BORED IN RECOVERY."

Reality:

Recovery opens up a world of possibilities that addiction had closed off. It allows you to tap into your innate potential, rediscover old passions, and develop new ones. Life in addiction might have been chaotic and exhausting, but recovery offers a chance to explore what truly makes you happy without the fog of addiction clouding your judgment.

Recovery helps you build and repair relationships, creating strong, genuine bonds that bring joy and contentment. With a newfound sense of purpose, you'll find there's no time to be bored. The path of recovery is about tapping into joy and excitement in a balanced, sustainable way, helping you grow into the person you were meant to be.

Actionable Step:

Explore new hobbies and interests. Join clubs, take classes, or volunteer. Filling your time with meaningful activities helps replace the void left by addiction.

Practical Advice:

Make a list of things you've always wanted to try but never had the chance to. Start exploring these interests now. By investing in your passions, you'll find that recovery is not boring but rather full of potential and excitement.

MYTH 6: "I CAN DO THIS ALONE."

Reality:

Recovery is not a solo journey. Support from family, friends, professionals, and groups like AA is vital. Think of it like being a professional athlete—they don't achieve their goals alone; they have a team of coaches, mentors, and supporters.

Addiction thrives in secrecy and isolation, so trying to go it alone plays into its hands. A support network provides accountability, encouragement, and a safety net when times get tough. Sharing your journey with others who've faced similar challenges offers strength, hope, and the reassurance that you're not alone.

Actionable Step:

Build a support network. Attend meetings, reach out to friends or family, and don't be afraid to ask for help when you need it. Recognize that strength comes from connection, not isolation.

Practical Advice:

Identify three people you can rely on during tough times—whether they are friends, family, or support group members. Keep their contact information handy and don't hesitate to reach out when you need a listening ear or advice.

MYTH 7: "TALKING ABOUT IT WILL MAKE IT HARDER."

Reality:

Talking about your recovery journey is incredibly beneficial. Sharing your experiences helps process emotions, making them more manageable. It builds connections with others, forming a safety net of support. Expressing vulnerabilities fosters emotional resilience, helping you overcome challenges with greater confidence.

Far from making things harder, talking about your feelings is at the heart of recovery. It clears confusion, builds bridges, and offers fresh perspectives. It's a powerful antidote to shame and a critical step towards healing, growth, and a fulfilling life.

"When we talk about our feelings, they become less overwhelming, less upsetting and less scary" - **Fred Rogers**

Actionable Step:

Find a safe space to share your story, whether it's with a therapist, a support group, or even a trusted friend. Talking helps you process your emotions and strengthens your resolve.

Practical Advice:

Start by writing about your experiences if talking feels too difficult at first. Gradually, share your story with someone you trust. You'll find that voicing your struggles lightens the burden and often leads to valuable insights and support from others.

DE-CLUTTERING FOR A SIMPLER RECOVERY PATH

I would like you to try something with me now. Visualise that this is the beginning of your recovery journey. In your mind really see what you see and feel what you feel using all of your senses.

You are walking into a super messy room. At first glance you just can't figure out where to start its overwhelming. This bedroom is a total mess! Chaos and unmanageability all around you. It looks like no one has cleaned it in a very long time. Clothes are everywhere - on the floor, over the chairs, hanging from the door, you name it. It's hard to even see the floor with all the stuff lying around. The air smells stale and dusty, and you can tell the room hasn't been aired out in a long time.

The bed stands as no sanctuary either. The air is heavy around the bed with the weight of years of neglect and sadness. The sheets and covers, wrinkled and faded, tell tales of better days long passed, now appearing aged and worn. The bed remains unmade, its pillows crushed, its blankets tossed carelessly at its foot. Each fold in the sheets and each dent in the pillows hold the echoes of restless, tormented nights still frozen in a state of unrest.

Dust is floating around, catching the little light coming through the dirty window. There are also random things scattered around, like old magazines with yellow pages, empty snack containers, old pizza boxes and empty bottles of booze still reeking of self-loathing, shame and isolation. This odour remains trapped inside, holding it as a reminder that this is your life. It's clear that this room has been neglected for a very long time. There is a claustrophobic feeling here that is clinging.

As you stand there behind you, you feel a soft breath of fresh air coming in through the door. Like a soft voice its whispers possibilities. It feels like a breath of hope and carries a faint but undeniable scent of opportunity, the chance to transform not only this room but your life and the path you are on. It ignites a spark within you, a spark that begins to glow and light up what was the overwhelming darkness of the task ahead. You begin to understand now that this disorder and unmanageability, a reflection of your inner turmoil, didn't accumulate overnight. It was a gradual build-up of neglect, each item a representation of choices made, paths taken, and experiences lived. Just as the mess has layers, so too will the process of sorting through it.

The seeds of a plan and some patience start to form in your mind, and you realise that the room (and your path to recovery) can become clean and clutter free. This fills you with hope and the glow becomes a beacon of clarity, it lights you up inside. You start to cultivate the seeds of the plan to begin the work.

RECOGNIZE THE MESS

The first step in recovery is acknowledging that there's a problem. Just as you stand in that messy room and say, "This place is a mess," you must also look at your life and admit that things have spiralled out of control. This is where the journey begins—by admitting powerlessness over your addiction, as the first step in the Twelve Steps of AA teaches us. It's a humbling realization that, like the clutter in the room, the chaos in your life has taken over, making it impossible to function normally. Imagine trying to find your keys or a favorite book in that chaotic room. It's nearly impossible, right? In the same way, when addiction controls our lives, it clutters everything, making it hard to see a way out. Stress and anxiety take over, and we can't see the wood for the trees. Admitting powerlessness isn't about defeat; it's about recognizing that the situation requires intervention. It's about saying, "I can't do this alone, and that's okay." This acknowledgment brings the gift of humility, allowing you to open up to the help you need.

DECIDE WHAT'S ESSENTIAL

Now, picture another room, one that's clean and uncluttered. It has only your favorite books, the clothes you wear often because they make you feel confident, and memories that bring a smile to your face. Which room feels better? The second one, of course. Just like these rooms, our lives can be filled with habits, activities, and relationships—some that enhance our lives, and others that simply clutter it. In recovery, it's crucial to distinguish between what helps and what hinders. Start by focusing on supportive habits, the ones that make you feel good and grounded, like a morning routine, journaling, or attending weekly support group meetings. These habits are like those comfy old shoes that, while worn, are dependable.

Next, identify the excess baggage. This could be habits or relationships that once seemed beneficial but now only add clutter, like late-night phone scrolling that disrupts your sleep, or a friend who downplays your recovery journey. It might also include hanging out with people who are still using or visiting places that tempt you back into old habits. To decide what to keep and what to let go of, take an honest inventory. Ask yourself, "Is this habit, activity, or relationship adding positive value to my life and recovery?" If the answer is no, it's time to reconsider its place in your life. Decluttering your space— both physically and emotionally—creates a refreshing, open space where you can breathe, grow, and thrive.

CREATING THE IDEAL ROOM

Once you've decided what to keep and what to let go of, it's time to arrange your room (and your life) in a way that supports your recovery. If an old, torn-up couch isn't working for you anymore, replace it with a new, comfy one.

The same goes for old habits or relationships that no longer serve you. This process may cause some discomfort and internal conflict, but it's essential for opening the door to a better life and a sustainable recovery.

Surround yourself with constructive habits and supportive people. Think of them as your favorite comfy chair or cherished photos that bring warmth to your room. These are the things and people you can rely on when times get tough, helping you stay on track and avoid falling back into old patterns.

SAFETY FEATURES

Just as a house is equipped with smoke alarms and locks to ensure safety, your journey in recovery necessitates its own form of protection. This protection isn't about erecting physical barriers, but about making wise choices that steer you clear of potential pitfalls. Embracing and maintaining healthy habits forms the cornerstone of this safeguarding strategy. Whether it's adhering to a regular exercise routine, engaging in mindfulness meditation, or ensuring a balanced diet, these habits build a robust foundation that keeps your recovery on stable ground. Additionally, surrounding yourself with people who genuinely care about your wellbeing is crucial. These individuals are more than just friends; they are vital components of your support system, offering encouragement and understanding when you need it most.

These healthy habits and positive relationships create a comprehensive safety net for your recovery. They act as vigilant sentinels, guarding against the relapse triggers and emotional upheavals that can so easily unsettle you. Just as the physical security in a home provides peace of mind, the practices and connections you cultivate in recovery offer emotional and psychological security. When you inevitably face challenges or setbacks, this safety net is there to catch you, providing the support and stability needed to regain your footing. Together, these elements not only protect your progress but also promote a resilient, sustained recovery grounded in care and intention.

THE PATH FORWARD

Deciding what's essential in recovery mirrors the process of decluttering a room. It involves making intentional, and often challenging, choices about what to keep in your life and what to let go. This process is not just about physical or emotional clutter, but about homing in on what genuinely benefits and enriches your life. By deliberately choosing habits, relationships, and activities that support your well-being, you create a living space—and a life—that allows for easier breathing and clearer thinking. This newfound clarity and purpose set the stage for a recovery journey marked by growth and simplicity, making each step forward more meaningful and focused.

As we clear the clutter that complicates life and recovery, we open up invaluable space for growth, joy, and discovery. This isn't just about making room physically but creating emotional and mental space that invites new opportunities for healing and happiness. Embracing simplicity in this way cultivates a richer, more fulfilling path in recovery, one where each moment is appreciated, and each small victory celebrated. By streamlining our environment and our choices, we're not just surviving in recovery; we're thriving, equipped with the clarity and drive to move forward with steadfast purpose and joy.

CHAPTER TWO SUMMARY

Complexity of Life and Recovery:

Life's complexity can make recovery seem daunting. However, simplifying our approach can light up the path to healing.

Dispelling Myths:

Seven common myths about recovery often create barriers. By debunking these myths, we can simplify our understanding of the recovery process.

- **Myth 1** - Need for Perfection: Recovery isn't about being perfect but making progress.

- **Myth 2 - Past Failures Define Us:** Previous setbacks don't doom us to failure. Like learning to ride a bike, persistence and learning from falls are key.

- **Myth 3 - Recovery Is Merely Quitting:** True recovery involves personal growth, wellness, and finding purpose, affecting all areas of life.

- **Myth 4 - Life Will Be Unmanageable Without Substances:** Initially daunting, facing life without substances allows for emotional growth and a deeper experience of life's highs and lows.

- **Myth 5 - Boredom in Recovery:** Recovery opens doors to rediscovering old passions and finding new interests, enriching life beyond the limitations of addiction.

- **Myth 6 - Going It Alone:** Recovery requires a support network. Attempting to recover alone plays into addiction's hands, and never ends well.

- **Myth 7 - Silence Is Easier:** Talking about struggles can make them more manageable. Sharing experiences helps process emotions and builds support. Acknowledging the mess, deciding what's essential, setting up our environment, and establishing safety measures are steps towards simplifying recovery.

Main Points of Chapter Two:

Simplifying the often-overwhelming journey of recovery by dispelling common myths. We focus on progress over perfection, learning from past attempts, the holistic nature of recovery, the value of facing life without substances, the opportunities for growth and enrichment, the necessity of support, and the power of sharing one's story. By understanding these key concepts, recovery can be viewed not as an insurmountable challenge but as a path toward a renewed, purposeful life.

CLARITY THROUGH MINIMALISM

Minimalism extends far beyond just owning fewer possessions; it's about living with intention. Think of it as choosing quality over quantity, curating your personal life museum by selecting items, relationships, and experiences that truly resonate with who you are and aspire to be. Minimalism isn't about avoiding challenges; rather, it's about facing them with clarity. Let's start simple. We will return to our messy room, close your eyes and feel what you feel and see what you see.

Imagine walking into a room and facing a closet bursting at the seams, stuffed with clothes that haven't been worn in years. Shoes spill out, and miscellaneous items gather dust at the bottom. It's a chaotic mess. Every time you need to find a particular shirt or pair of shoes, it turns into a full-blown treasure hunt. The clutter isn't just physical; it's mentally taxing too. The chaos makes you feel overwhelmed and stressed.

Now let's change that scenario.

You've decided to dedicate a weekend to tackling that chaotic closet. You pull everything out, piling it onto the bed. One by one, you evaluate each item. Does that sweater still fit? Do you even like those shoes anymore? Why are you holding onto that single sock without a pair? As you sift through, you start discarding items that no longer serve a purpose. Some clothes might be donated, others sold or recycled, and a few just thrown out.

After this thorough cleanse, you're left with only the items you genuinely love and use. Your closet is now neat and organized. Every time you open it, you see things that bring you joy and make your life easier. Getting dressed in the morning becomes a breeze, and the weight of unnecessary clutter is lifted. It's liberating. This isn't just about a closet; it's a metaphor for our lives.

APPLYING MINIMALISM TO LIFE: THE POWER OF INTENTIONAL LIVING

Minimalism isn't merely about decluttering physical spaces; it's about stripping away anything that doesn't add value to our life. Think beyond the cluttered closet or overflowing drawers—consider the toxic relationships that drain your energy, the unfulfilling tasks that consume our time, and the mindless activities that distract us from our true passions. By consciously removing this excess baggage, we create space for what truly matters. This could mean more quality time with loved ones, the freedom to pursue hobbies that ignite our spirit, or simply the peace that comes from a life lived with intention. It's about making deliberate choices that align with our values, allowing us to focus on what brings joy and fulfillment.

Minimalism is like a spring cleaning for your entire existence. It's about tidying up not just our physical surroundings but also our routines, relationships, and even our thoughts. Imagine the liberation of releasing obligations that no longer serve us, or the clarity that comes from a mind free of constant clutter. The result? A life that feels more focused, fulfilling, and free. By eliminating the unnecessary, we open up room for growth, happiness, and authentic connections. Minimalism empowers you to live deliberately, appreciate the simple pleasures, and find contentment in the essentials, leading to a richer and more meaningful life.

MINIMALISM AND RECOVERY - WHAT'S THE CONNECTION.

Both minimalism and recovery focus on transformation and renewal. In recovery, we rebuild our lives by letting go of harmful habits and mindsets, embracing new, healthier ones. Whether recovering from addiction, trauma, or any other life-altering experience, the path often involves shedding the old to make room for the new. Just as a minimalist declutters their physical space to create a more peaceful environment, someone in recovery declutters their mental and emotional space to foster healing and growth.

Applying minimalism to recovery allows us to focus on what truly helps us heal. By stripping away distractions and unnecessary burdens, we can better see the path ahead. We let go of the negative and hold on to the positive. Just as minimalism encourages us to keep only items that add value to our lives, recovery teaches us to embrace habits and thoughts that benefit us. This might involve adopting new routines, cultivating supportive relationships, or engaging in activities that promote well-being.

In the process of recovery, we often find that our lives have become cluttered with negative influences, unhealthy relationships, and unproductive habits. Minimalism invites us to assess these aspects critically. We ask ourselves: Does this relationship uplift me or hold me back? Does this habit contribute to my well-being or hinder my progress? By consciously choosing to eliminate what's detrimental, we create space for healing and positive growth.

Both minimalism and recovery show us that life becomes clearer and more meaningful when we focus on what's important. When we remove the noise and chaos, we're able to appreciate the simple joys and find contentment in the present moment. By getting rid of the extra clutter, whether physical or emotional, we can live a more focused, happier life. We open up space not just in our homes, but in our hearts and minds, allowing us to grow and thrive.

Embracing minimalism can reduce the stress and anxiety that often accompany recovery. A simplified environment can promote calmness and clarity, making it easier to maintain sobriety or overcome past traumas. It helps us to be more mindful and present, recognizing and appreciating the value of each moment without being overwhelmed by unnecessary distractions.

Minimalism and recovery are intertwined journeys that lead us towards a life of intentionality and purpose. By letting go of what no longer serves us, we make room for new experiences, healthier relationships, and personal growth. Together, they empower us to rebuild our lives on a foundation of simplicity and authenticity, leading to lasting happiness and fulfillment.

STARTING FRESH WITH MINIMALISM- MOVING FROM CLUTTERED SPACES TO CLEAR MINDS

Imagine your life as an old family home—full of memories and stories, but also full of clutter. Over the years, every nook and cranny has collected items—boxes under the staircase, piles in the attic, and heaps in the garage. It's like a library of past choices: books you never read, outfits you hoped to fit into, gadgets you were sure you'd use but never did. Each object represents a decision made—some good, some impulsive, some regrettable. Now, imagine relocating to a sleek, modern apartment in the heart of the city, a place with crisp lines and limited space. There's no way every box from your old home will fit. This move isn't just physical; it's symbolic. It's a call to reflect on what truly matters. Every item you pack forces you to decide, "Does this serve a purpose? Is this a token of joy or a bind of regret? Is its emotional weight worth the physical space it occupies?"

As you sort through your belongings, you might find items that evoke guilt or regret—like that outfit you bought on a whim but never wore, or those ambitious books that stand as silent judges on your shelf. Do these things still deserve a place in your life? On the other hand, you also discover treasures—

photos, handwritten notes, keepsakes from loved ones. These items anchor you to cherished memories and undoubtedly earn their place in your new life.

This process mirrors the essence of minimalism and recovery: it's not just about discarding objects; it's about shedding the emotional baggage of past choices, mistakes, and regrets. It's about embracing what truly enriches your soul and letting go of what drags you down. Minimalism isn't about living with the bare minimum; it's about consciously deciding what gets to stay in your life and what doesn't. By doing so, you make space for things that truly add value, happiness, and meaning to your life.

MINIMALISM – DESIGNING A SYMPHONY OF PURPOSE

Visualize that you're standing in a grand concert hall that represents your current life. The orchestra isn't in sync—some notes are jarring, creating a racket, while others are soothing and harmonious. This discrepancy mirrors the clutter in your life—the noise, the distractions, the overwhelming chaos that drowns out the clarity and purpose you seek.

Recovery and minimalism function as expert conductors, guiding each aspect of your life to produce a melody that resonates with meaning and clarity. Consider the clamor of negativity as the overwhelming sound of an out-of-tune instrument—distracting, persistent, and unsettling. Both recovery and minimalism inspire us to turn down the volume on these overwhelming frequencies, muting the chaos and amplifying the harmonies of positivity.

Merging recovery and minimalism isn't just about tidying up; it's like a complete renovation of your life's concert hall. This transformation isn't about merely dusting off the seats or sweeping the stage. It's about restructuring the acoustics, ensuring every note, every emotion, every experience is heard with clarity and purpose. It's not just about discarding the noise but orchestrating a symphony where each note, each instrument, contributes to a larger, purposeful melody. In this renovated concert hall, every day isn't just another routine performance, but a masterful composition played with intention and depth. Every chord, every silence, and every crescendo is deliberate and meaningful, leading toward a life lived fully, richly, and authentically.

THE IMPORTANCE OF DECLUTTERING PHYSICAL AND MENTAL SPACES FOR ENHANCED RECOVERY

Sobriety demands immense focus, determination, and clarity. While refraining from substance use is a significant part of this journey, true transformation involves holistic changes in both your environment and mindset. That's where decluttering—both physical and mental—becomes crucial. Recovery can be likened to navigating through a dense forest. To find our way out, we need clear markers, a well-trodden path, and the removal of any obstructions. Just as we clear away brambles or fallen logs blocking our way in the forest, in recovery, it's essential to eliminate anything that might hamper our progress. This includes tangible temptations and the intangible burdens we carry—old grudges, past mistakes, unresolved traumas, and the clutter surrounding your daily life.

Our living space often reflects our internal state. A cluttered room can mirror a cluttered mind, filled with anxieties, fears, and confusion. Similarly, a mind weighed down by negative thoughts and memories can manifest in our physical world as chaos and disorder. When embarking on the challenging path of recovery, it's vital to address both aspects. Decluttering, both physically and mentally, isn't just about creating space; it's about creating an environment that nurtures and supports the healing process.

PHYSICAL SPACES AND SOBRIETY: REMOVING TRIGGERS

Every physical space holds energy—positive, negative, or neutral. These spaces can act as emotional triggers, loaded with memories of moments of weakness or indulgence. Every object, which might seem harmless to an outsider, could be an IED (Innocuous Emotional Detonation)—a loaded emotional trigger waiting to be set off. For instance, the couch where we spent our darkest moments or the scent of a particular room that reminds us of a place where we often indulged in our addiction. These aren't just "things"; they're repositories of memories, emotions, and stories. Removing these triggers is like detoxifying our environment. It's not merely about decluttering; it's about consciously purging spaces of negative energy and memories, signifying a break from the chains of the past.

THE ACTIVE ROLE OF SPACES IN RECOVER

Physical spaces aren't passive; they play an active role in our healing journey. Every room, every corner, every piece of furniture tells a story. They are silent witnesses to our past actions, joys, and regrets. When we are in recovery, space can be a constant reminder of past habits or even past failures. However, changing these spaces, decluttering them, or rearranging them can also reflect a new story — a story of resilience, change, and hope. By actively reshaping our spaces, we're rewriting our story. We make the choice to become the author of our own future story.

Spaces can be set up to serve as sanctuaries, offering peace, solace, and safety. On our recovery journey, having a dedicated space that feels safe, where we can retreat, reflect, and relax, can be invaluable. This sanctuary might be a room filled with books, a corner with soft lighting and comfortable cushions, or a garden space with fragrant flowers and calming water features. It can be a bench in a local park at a particular time of day where we can sit amongst nature and just be. By establishing these sanctuaries, we can create unique spaces shaped to our personal needs and preferences, promoting relaxation, introspection, and healing during our recovery journey.

ORGANIZED SPACES FOR MENTAL CLARITY

Our environment has a major impact on our mental state. A cluttered room often reflects or exacerbates a cluttered mind, while an organized space can instill a sense of order and calm, providing clarity of thought. This clarity is invaluable in recovery, offering a respite from the chaos that addiction or trauma might have brought into our life. Maintaining an organized space requires consistent effort. The daily act of making our bed might seem mundane, but it sets a positive tone for the day. It's a small act of control, a tiny victory that strengthens our discipline over time. Such repetitive, beneficial actions serve as daily affirmations of our commitment to recovery.

Organized spaces also facilitate the creation of "habit loops." A habit loop consists of a cue, a routine, and a reward. For example, seeing a neatly arranged meditation corner (cue) might prompt us to engage in a ten-minute meditation session (routine). The resulting calm and accomplishment serve as the reward, reinforcing the habit. Over time, these loops become deeply ingrained, supporting sustained positive practices.

Designated spaces for activities like reading or exercise act as daily reminders of our commitment to recovery and well-being. These spaces silently communicate, "This is important. This deserves space in my life." By having specific spots for particular activities, we reduce the number of daily decisions we need to make, minimizing decision fatigue—a precious resource in recovery. Each completed activity in these designated spaces adds a link to our chain of positive habits. Over time, the fear of breaking this chain can motivate continuity in practice. For instance, if we've journaled every morning for 50 days straight in our writing spot, we're more likely to push through on day 51, even if we're not in the mood, simply to keep the chain going.

Starting with one organized space or habit often creates a ripple effect, inspiring organization and discipline in other areas of our life. Experiencing the benefits of a tidy meditation corner might encourage us to organize our kitchen, promoting better eating habits, or establish a nighttime reading routine, further supporting our development in recovery. In simple words, having a tidy and well-organized place is not just about making things look good; it helps and encourages us to stay sober and improve ourself. A clean space reminds us every day to stick to our goals and make better choices, aiding us on our journey to a better life.

CHAPTER THREE SUMMARY

Essence of Minimalism:

Minimalism is about living intentionally, choosing quality over quantity in all aspects of life. It's about focusing on what truly matters and letting go of the rest.

The Messy Closet:

A cluttered closet symbolizes the chaos and stress caused by holding onto unnecessary items. Cleaning out the closet and keeping only what brings joy and serves a purpose mirrors the minimalist approach to life.

Applying Minimalism to Life:

Minimalism encourages eliminating physical objects, toxic relationships, and unfulfilling activities from our lives, creating space for meaningful interactions, passions, and simplicity.

Minimalism and Recovery:

Both minimalism and recovery involve transformative journeys that require letting go of harmful habits and focusing on what aids healing and promotes a healthy lifestyle.

Starting Fresh:

Moving to a new, smaller space forces a re-evaluation of possessions and priorities, much like the minimalist approach to life encourages focusing on essentials and personal growth.

Decluttering as a Symbol:

Decluttering physical and mental spaces is crucial in recovery, allowing for a clearer path forward and removing obstacles that hinder progress.

The Role of Physical Spaces in Recovery:

Changing your environment to reflect your journey of change and hope can significantly impact recovery by removing triggers and creating supportive spaces.

Organized Spaces for Mental Clarity:

Organized and purposeful spaces calm the mind and promote habits that support recovery, illustrating the psychological benefits of a minimalist environment.

Designing Spaces for Recovery:

Creating specific areas for activities like meditation or exercise reinforces positive habits and reduces decision fatigue, aiding in the recovery process.

Main Points of Chapter Three:

Adopting a minimalist lifestyle can significantly enhance the recovery process. By intentionally choosing to keep only what brings us joy and serves a purpose, we can declutter not just our physical environment but also our mind and life. This simplicity and clarity provide a solid foundation for focusing on recovery and personal growth.

BACK TO BASICS

In today's fast paced world it's easy to get lost in the chaos, especially when battling an addiction. The Alcoholics Anonymous (AA) program offers a beacon of hope by introducing basic principles that can lead us out of the darkness. The heart of the Alcoholics Anonymous (AA) program lies in its 12 Steps. These aren't just guidelines to quit drinking, they're a framework for a complete life overhaul. The beauty of the AA program isn't just in its structured approach but in its simplicity. It calls on us to take a hard look at ourselves, to admit our flaws, to seek guidance, and to make amends. It doesn't offer a magical solution but emphasises the power of human connection, honesty, and spiritual growth.

At the core of this transformative journey is the idea of 'surrender.' It's about recognising that we don't have all the answers and that sometimes, admitting powerlessness can be the first step to gaining real, sustainable strength. This might sound paradoxical, but there's a powerful truth to it. It's only when we let go of our stubbornness and pride that we open ourselves up to guidance, be it from a higher power, a mentor, or a supportive community. Another central element is accountability. The 12 Step program pushes us to confront our actions, our choices, and their repercussions head-on. While it's often painful to revisit the past, especially the parts we're not proud of, doing so is essential. This process of self-reflection and acknowledgment helps to break the chains of denial and sets the stage for genuine transformation.

Then there's the emphasis on community. Alcoholics Anonymous underlines the importance of shared experiences and mutual support. Addiction is isolating, making us feel trapped in a bubble of guilt, shame, and loneliness. The AA community acts as a lifeline, reminding us that we're not alone in our struggles and that recovery is not just possible but achievable. In the rooms we share our stories of failure, resilience, and triumph. These stories offer us both cautionary tales and sources of inspiration.

But why go back to basics when there are a whole raft of modern therapies and treatments available? The answer lies in the long term effectiveness of these basic principles. In an age of information overload and constant distractions, stripping down to the basics provides clarity. As described earlier it's like decluttering a cluttered room, by removing all the excess, we can clearly see what's important. For me personally I have yet to come across an alternative that works as well as the Twelve Step Programme.

The Twelve Steps of Alcoholics Anonymous provide a structured yet compassionate path to recovery, guiding us from the initial acknowledgment of our addiction to achieving sustained sobriety and spiritual growth. These steps involve admitting powerlessness over alcohol, seeking the support of a higher power, engaging in deep self-reflection, making amends for past wrongs, and ultimately, using personal transformation to help others on their recovery journey. Together, they form a holistic framework for healing that emphasizes honesty, humility, and the power of community.

In the following sections, we'll delve into the Twelve Steps of the AA program, explore how this focus on basic values can lead to massive changes, and offer guidance on how we can incorporate these core principles into our everyday life. Whether we're in the height of addiction, in recovery, or simply looking for a path to personal growth, these principles have a universal significance.

ADMITTING POWERLESSNESS

Step 1 – We admitted we were powerless over alcohol and our lives had become unmanageable.

In the first step of AA, we come to terms with the fact that alcohol controls us more than we control it, and this is both a tough and freeing thing to do. This step is all about getting past our ego, which we've let run our lives for too long. Our ego made us think we were protecting ourselves, but it was really just feeding off our bitterness, shame, and anger. Accepting we can't control our addiction isn't admitting defeat; it's being really honest with ourselves. It's seeing that the idea of having control is just something we tell ourselves to keep going in a harmful cycle. Facing up to our addiction is the crucial first step toward finding real answers. Denial is a significant hurdle in this process, acting as the ego's guard, preventing growth and self-awareness. Common signs of denial include rationalizing excessive drinking, minimizing its consequences, blaming external circumstances or others for one's drinking behavior, and continuing to drink despite clear evidence of mounting personal and professional problems. Other signs include feeling isolated or defensive about drinking habits and dismissing concerns expressed by friends or family. Identifying these signs of denial can be a crucial first step towards acknowledging the need for change and seeking help, marking the beginning of a journey toward recovery and a clearer, more hopeful life.

This step is more than admitting the obvious problems like health issues or money troubles caused by drinking. It's about understanding how alcohol has messed up our relationships, squandered opportunities, self-esteem, and led to many regrets. Step One changes everything. It's about facing the hard truth of how alcohol has wrecked parts of our lives. This honesty is what starts the healing process, helps us grow, and gives us a new sense of direction. It's the beginning of a journey that takes us from a messed-up life to one that's clear and hopeful, a life rebuilt through recovery.

FINDING HOPE IN A GREATER POWER

***Step Two - We came to believe that a Power greater
than ourselves could restore us to sanity.***

Step Two is really special and makes us think hard. It goes beyond just the idea of spirituality and brings in a sense of hope, trust, and being humble. When we're dealing with addiction, we often feel really down, isolated, ashamed and guilty. This step offers a different way to look at things: it suggests we're not fighting this battle by ourselves and that maybe there's a bigger, kinder force that can help us get our minds clear again. This "Higher Power" idea means different things to different people. It could be a religious figure, the strength we get from being in a group like AA, the universe, nature, or just a personal spiritual belief. The main point is realising there's something bigger than us that can help.

Choosing to believe in a Higher Power in Step Two changes our outlook hugely. It shifts us from feeling all alone to having hope and seeing that we can change. This step tells us that even though we've lost our way, there's still something out there that believes in us, even if we're having a hard time believing in ourselves. The step talks about getting back to "sanity" instead of just "sobriety," meaning it's about more than just not drinking or using drugs. It's about getting our minds clear and making good decisions again.

The concept of Higher Power varies widely among individuals—it can be a religious figure, the collective strength of a support group like AA, the interconnectedness of nature, personal values, or even the universe itself. Embracing this concept means recognizing that we are not alone in our struggle, allowing for external spiritual or communal support to guide us towards making clear and healthy decisions. This step encourages openness to help, vulnerability, and a shift from isolation to a supported journey of recovery, fostering growth through a belief system that resonates on a personal level.

Step Two is also about finding strength in admitting we don't have all the answers and might need help from outside ourselves. This isn't about giving up; it's about being open to more help and understanding that it's okay to be vulnerable. It's about moving from a place where we have been uncomfortably comfortable to a place where we're okay with being comfortably uncomfortable because it means we're growing. This step is like a light showing us the way and asking us to be humble, to look into our spiritual side, to see that healing can come from outside ourselves, and to trust in the path we're on.

HANDING OVER THE REINS

***Step Three - Made a decision to turn our will and our lives
over to the care of God as we understood Him.***

Step Three is a big turning point on the road to getting better. It's all about starting to see life and recovery in a new way. This step means being open to trust, being humble, and ready for big changes. Recovery isn't just about stopping the use of alcohol or drugs; it's also about totally changing how we think and deal with problems. In this step, we admit that we can't control everything and start to trust in something bigger than us. It's recognising that our addiction has been making all the decisions and now it's time for a new direction.

Practicing Step Three of the AA program involves incorporating daily affirmations and intentions to deepen our connection to a Higher Power and cultivate a new approach to life. Daily affirmations such as "Today, I choose trust over fear" or "I am open to guidance and wisdom beyond my own" help reinforce the decision to surrender control and foster a mindset of openness and readiness for the day ahead. These affirmations are a simple yet powerful way to start each day with a clear intention of trusting a higher guidance.

In addition to affirmations, setting specific daily intentions that align with the qualities sought from a Higher Power, like patience, courage, or wisdom, can be highly effective. For instance, an intention might be "Today, I will seek patience in my interactions and listen more than I speak" or "I will look for opportunities to practice kindness as guided by my Higher Power." Regular meditation or prayer sessions also play a crucial role in maintaining this spiritual connection, allowing for quiet reflection and an opportunity to receive guidance. These practices ensure we remain committed to our recovery path, promoting continuous personal growth and spiritual development throughout their journey.

Choosing to be guided by a Higher Power is a conscious decision, not just giving up. It's like a climber trusting an expert guide, realising that this Higher Power knows better than us how to get through recovery. It means being brave enough to ask for help and being open to new ideas and ways. It's about listening to others who can help and being guided by spiritual or philosophical beliefs. Step Three is really about learning to be humble, understanding that our addiction messed with our judgment, and accepting that there's a lot we can learn from others. It's about stepping back, listening, and being ready for the hard but rewarding work ahead in our journey to healing and recovery.

FEARLESS SOUL-SEARCHING

Step 4: Made a searching and fearless moral inventory of ourselves.

Step Four is all about deep and honest self-reflection, a crucial part of getting better. It's where we really look at ourselves and the impact of our actions. This step means facing up to the truth, even if it's tough. It's more than just admitting to bad habits; it's about getting to the bottom of why we did what we did. This could be due to fear, insecurity, shame or pain. Understanding all this is key to healing and making sure we don't fall back into old ways. It sets us up to make things right with people we've hurt.

The easiest person to lie to in the world is ourself. We make up stories to avoid facing hard truths. Doing a thorough and honest review of our past – our actions, thoughts, and reasons – helps break through this self-deception. We look for patterns like selfishness or dishonesty that are part of our addiction. This step helps us get better at understanding and managing our emotions, and it's tough. It means accepting hard truths about ourselves. Writing all this down can really help. It's like letting out all the built-up emotional tension we've been carrying inside. Having someone like a sponsor or counsellor with us in this process can offer the support and insight we need. I cannot stress enough the importance of being kind to yourself while you do this. It's not about beating ourselves up over past mistakes. It's about learning from them. Seeing our actions in a balanced way helps us grow as people. This step is about changing from who we used to be to who we are meant to be. It's a big part of healing and sets us up for lasting change and personal growth.

I would like to share the brief story of Marie who faced her past actions by completing a thorough Step Four, and the incredibly positive impact it had on her recovery journey. Marie embarked on a transformative journey with Step Four of her recovery program, committing to a thorough moral inventory of her actions and underlying motivations. This process involved deep introspection and honesty, where she faced the uncomfortable truths of her past, including sabotaged relationships and missed opportunities. Through detailed writing and reflection, she uncovered patterns of behavior linked to deep-seated fears and insecurities. With the support of her sponsor, Marie processed her findings, which not only lifted the burden of her past but also brought clarity and peace. This reflective exercise allowed her to identify emotional triggers and their connections to her addictive behaviors, marking a pivotal shift in her recovery.

Moving confidently into Step Five, Marie felt empowered to admit her wrongs to herself, her confidant, and a higher power. This step of vulnerability and humility was key to building trust and fostering connection, crucial components for her ongoing healing and personal growth. By embracing her imperfections and accepting external help, Marie paved a new path towards a hopeful and more self-aware future.

CONFESSION

Step Five- Admitted to God, to ourselves, and to another human being the exact nature of our wrongs.

Step Five is a profound step toward strengthening self-acceptance, requiring us not just to recognize our past mistakes but to genuinely come to terms with them. It invites us to take control of our narrative, including the parts we are not proud of, and to acknowledge that our past does not determine our future. Admitting our wrongs to a Higher Power, as we understand it, serves as an acknowledgment of our imperfections and our reliance on something greater than ourselves. This act of humility extends to sharing our deepest faults with a trusted individual like a sponsor, confidant, or spiritual advisor, building trust and mitigating feelings of isolation. It demands the courage to reveal our true selves, with all our imperfections laid bare.

Choosing the right person to confide in is crucial, as discussing our darkest moments and deepest shames can trigger intense emotional responses. Afterall we are baring our soul to another heartbeat. A spiritual advisor or therapist can provide a secure environment for these revelations, offering essential guidance, understanding, and validation. Their support is invaluable in helping us reinterpret our past actions with compassion and empathy, facilitating emotional healing and personal growth. This process is not just about unburdening but about transforming the experience into a shared journey toward recovery, ensuring it is not a path walked alone but a collective stride toward a brighter, more open-hearted future.

Ultimately, Step Five paves the way for significant emotional liberation and self-improvement. Sharing our burdens opens us up to new levels of understanding and kindness toward ourselves, enabling us to grow and become more authentic. This step reassures us that our past errors do not define us; rather, they present an opportunity to create a more promising future, cultivating a mindset geared toward continual growth. It prepares us for sustained recovery and profound personal development. Like Fred Rogers said, talking about our feelings makes them less scary and overwhelming, leading us to a life that's more hopeful and less burdened by our past.

"Anything that's human is mentionable, and anything that is mentionable can be more manageable. When we can talk about our feelings, they become less overwhelming, less upsetting, and less scary. The people we trust with that important talk can help us know that we are not alone." – **Fred Rogers**

GETTING READY FOR TRANSFORMATION

Step 6 - Were entirely ready to have God remove all these defects of character.

Step Six is about getting ready for big changes in ourselves. After figuring out our personal faults in earlier steps, this step is about mentally and emotionally preparing to let go of these negative traits. It's more than just knowing what's wrong; it's about truly being prepared and willing to work on these issues. This means opening ourselves up to help that goes beyond just our own willpower, like leaning on a higher power or the support from our AA group. We're creating a space inside ourselves where real change can happen, being open to that change, and realising that true transformation starts from within.

Letting go of character defects is far from easy. Even if they're hurting us, these habits might have been our coping mechanisms or a big part of who we are for a long time. It can be scary to let them go because it might feel like we're losing a part of ourselves. These features might have been our emotional armour, protecting us when we felt exposed, or masks we put on to handle life's tough moments. But eventually, what used to help us can end up being harmful, like when our ego gets too big and starts causing more problems than it solves. It's important to realize that this overblown ego can try to sabotage our efforts to change by feeding us lies and undermining our growth. It requires us to be ready and willing to let go of deeply ingrained character defects with patience and humility. This step extends beyond recognizing personal faults; it involves preparing mentally and emotionally to release negative traits that have served as coping mechanisms or emotional armor, even though they may feel like integral parts of our identity. To identify these defects, we can use tools such as journaling to track recurring behaviors and progress, reflecting on how these traits result in negative outcomes. Engaging with a higher power, mentors, or support groups can provide necessary support and accountability. Cultivating gratitude is also vital, as it shifts focus from deficiencies to positive changes and growth. We should approach this gradual journey towards change with self-compassion, recognizing that letting go of old habits is challenging but essential for moving forward into better things.

Step Six is about letting go and putting our trust in something greater than ourselves. It's about surrendering and also taking responsibility for our actions. We need to believe that shedding these negative attributes will lead us to a healthier and happier life. This step encourages us to embrace humility and gratitude. We're acknowledging our limits and being open to learning and growing. Humility isn't about thinking less of ourselves, we are not putting ourselves down. It's about having an honest view of who we are. Gratitude shifts our focus from what we lack to appreciating what we have and the progress we've made. It's a step towards a life of abundance. This change in perspective weakens the grip of our oversized ego and opens us up more to change. So, Step Six isn't just about getting rid of the bad stuff; it's about moving forward into a more positive and fulfilling life.

ASKING FOR CHANGE

Step Seven- Humbly ask Him to remove our shortcomings.

Step Seven is all about getting humble and using that humility to change and grow. It means admitting that we can't do everything on our own and need some extra help. This isn't just about trying to fix our bad habits; it's a deep dive into understanding why we do things like drink too much or use drugs. It's saying goodbye to our oversized egos that get in the way of getting better. When we drop our pride and ask for help, it's like we're giving up on the old, harmful ways and ready to start fresh with healthier habits.

The idea of a Higher Power in this step can mean different things for each of us. It could be a spiritual thing, the support we get from our AA group, or something else that guides us. This step is a constant process where we keep admitting our faults and looking for guidance to get better. It's not a one-time thing; it's a part of our daily life in recovery. Being humble and recognizing our flaws helps us become more resilient, patient, and understanding. This step deepens our connection to our higher power and gives us comfort and strength as we recover. It's crucial for staying sober in the long run because it keeps us focused on fixing our weaknesses and staying open to change.

Incorporating prayer and meditation is essential for fostering humility and enhancing spiritual connections, which are vital for personal growth. Starting each day with a Daily Gratitude Prayer helps shift focus from deficiencies to appreciating life's abundance, thereby promoting humility. Utilizing guided meditations focused on humility can deepen our understanding and acceptance of its role in recovery. Ending the day with a Reflection Prayer allows for introspection on moments of humility and identification of areas for improvement, further reinforcing our commitment to personal transformation.

Mindfulness meditation enhances awareness of present and reduces impulsivity and compulsions, crucial for maintaining an open and humble attitude. When we feel overwhelmed, a Surrender Prayer can reiterate our reliance on a Higher Power, asking for relief from our burdens and guidance in transformation. Additionally, engaging in Service Meditation by visualizing positive impacts on others strengthens the link between personal recovery and selfless behavior. These practices, integrated into our daily routines, significantly support the journey through Step Seven, enhancing our humility and readiness for change.

MAKING AMENDS

***Step Eight -Making a list of all persons we've harmed
and becoming willing to set things right.***

Step Eight is challenging but really important. It's where we list out all the people we hurt while we were addicted and get ready to fix those wrongs. We have to think back on our actions and how they affected others, which is pretty tough and requires us to be honest and brave. We need to make a complete list of everyone we hurt, including ourselves, because sometimes we forget how much we hurt ourselves too. Then we organize this list into groups based on when and how it's best to make amends, always remembering to take our time and think things through.

Forgiveness is a significant part of Step Eight. It's about forgiving other people and also forgiving ourselves. We often carry a lot of guilt and shame for what we did in the past. This step is filled with deep ideas like being honest, brave, willing to change, taking responsibility, being humble, and showing compassion. By letting go of bitterness and resentments, we free ourselves from our past and help our recovery. And when we forgive, we're not just helping ourselves; we're transmitting good energy that can help other people too.

To get through Step Eight, we will need to reflect a lot, write things down, talk to our sponsor or another confidant, or find other ways to get support. We need to be really thorough and honest with ourselves. We find that Step Eight is not a onetime exercise we may have to come back to this step later as we face new challenges. The ultimate goal is not just to amend past wrongs but to cultivate an environment of growth and healing, and just like cultivating a garden we must continuously tend to it.

This step is all about owning up to what we've done in the past and getting ready to fix things. It's a step full of courage, understanding, love, and forgiveness, and it's a big part of healing and growing. Making amends is more than just saying sorry; it's a way to rebuild our lives and keep growing in our sobriety.

REPARATION AND RESTITUTION

Step Nine - Made direct amends to such people wherever possible, except when to do so would injure them or others.

Step Nine is all about action. We set out to try to make things right and repair the damage we have caused to others and ourselves. This step is really personal and different for everyone, depending on what they did in the past and how it affected others. The main point is to own up to what we've done and take full responsibility, which is really important for healing, not just for ourselves but for those we've hurt too. This is not easy nor is it meant to be.

Step Nine isn't always simple. Sometimes, trying to make things right might do more harm than good, like bringing back painful memories or causing new problems. That's why we have to think carefully about each situation, sometimes getting advice from a sponsor or counsellor. The step is all about not making things worse while trying to make amends. This careful approach is especially important in sensitive situations where reaching out might unexpectedly hurt someone. We need to be conscious that in our enthusiasm to fix the wrongs of the past we don't create a situation that causes pain and suffering to another. This requires a delicate balance between seeking forgiveness and not reopening old wounds. It is vital we approach this step with sensitivity.

When direct contact is likely to reopen old wounds, alternative methods such as writing an unsent letter allow us to express remorse and confront personal feelings without risking further damage. Additionally, making indirect amends through positive community contributions and acts of kindness can also fulfill the step's objectives. These methods not only facilitate personal growth and responsibility but also ensure that the process of making amends remains constructive and aligned with the broader goals of recovery and self-improvement.

What's really important about Step Nine is that it's not just about fixing our past mistakes; it's also about our own growth and change. To make amends, we have to face hard truths, be humble, and learn to understand others better. It's not just about getting forgiveness or fixing relationships; it's about changing ourselves for the better. This step is about committing to be honest and responsible. We must not make the assumption that our amends will be accepted in all cases, they may not and in these situations, we must accept and be grateful that we at least had the opportunity to try. While it's about fixing things with others, it's also about growing ourselves, knowing that getting better and making positive changes is a crucial part of the continuous journey of recovery.

CONTINUOUS SELF-ASSESSMENT

Step 10 - Continued to take personal inventory and when we were wrong promptly admitted it.

Step 10 is all about keeping a regular check on ourselves and being quick to admit when we mess up. It's different from the deep dive we do in Step Four.

Here, it's more about staying on top of things every day. Think of it like a daily self-check-in. Each day, we take a moment to think about how we acted, what we thought, and how we behaved. It's about spotting any negative stuff early on, like bad habits or hurtful actions, and dealing with them before they get out of hand. This step keeps us from falling back into old ways and helps us stay on track with our recovery. It's not just about avoiding big mistakes; it's also about fine-tuning our daily actions to keep growing as individuals.

I do my daily inventory in the evening. I take ten minutes out on my own and reflect back over the day, how did I show up today, where my behaviors and actions aligned with my values? Did I offend or was I short with someone? Do I need to make an amends to that person? Did I offer my support, or did I attend to someone who was struggling? These are some of the questions we can all ask of ourselves; it keeps us grounded and aligned to our mission.

In this step, the big ticket is being able to say, *"I was wrong"* and really mean it. That can take a lot of courage to own up to our mistakes without making excuses. Just think on that for a second! This honesty stops guilt and resentment from building up, both in us and in our relationships. It's a key part of keeping things straight with the people in our lives and with ourselves. Also, by practising this every day, we get better at understanding who we are – what we're good at and what we still need to work on. This ongoing self-improvement is crucial for staying sober and really improves our emotional wellbeing. We get better at handling stress and all sorts of feelings without falling back into old, harmful patterns. In essence, Step 10 is about making this whole process of self-reflection and owning up to our mistakes a regular part of our lives. It's what keeps us moving forward and improving, making sure our recovery is something we live every day.

STRENGTHENING THE CONNECTION

Step 11- Sought through prayer and meditation to improve our conscious contact with God as we understood Him, praying only for knowledge of His will for us and the power to carry that out.

Step 11 is about deepening our spiritual connection in a way that makes sense to each of us as individuals. For me personally it is not about religion; it's more about finding my own way to connect with something bigger than myself. This step suggests using prayer and meditation to improve this connection. Prayer here isn't just about asking for things we want; it's more about trying to understand what a higher power (whatever that means to each of us) wants for us and asking for the strength to follow that path. Some of us may do this through traditional religious prayers, while others may find quiet reflection or mindfulness exercises more helpful.

For those of us seeking to deepen this spiritual engagement, a wealth of resources are available. Books such as The Serenity Prayer by Reinhold Niebuhr, and Meditations for the Twelve Step Program by Friends In Recovery offer insightful reflections that align with the principles of recovery. Apps like Headspace and Insight Timer provide guided meditations and mindfulness exercises tailored to enhance spiritual awareness and connection. Additionally, online communities and local support groups tailored to recovery can offer a space for shared experiences and mutual encouragement. Whether it's through reading, using technology, or participating in community gatherings, these tools can help us explore and strengthen tour spiritual paths, ensuring their journey in recovery is both grounded and uplifting.

The main purpose of step 11 is twofold.

First: It's about getting clearer on what we believe our higher power wants for us—figuring out the right thing to do in our life, based on higher principles or bigger goals. It's like trying to tune in to a guidance system that's not just about our own personal wants and needs.

Second: It's about asking for the strength and courage to actually do those things. It's one thing to know what's right, but often quite another to have the guts to follow through. This step is acknowledging that sometimes, we need a little extra help to live up to our own ideals.

In short, Step 11 is a reminder to keep working on our spiritual life as part of our recovery. It's an encouragement to find and keep up a practice that helps us stay connected to our higher power, in whatever form that takes for each of us. This isn't just about staying sober; it's about leading a life that's guided by a sense of purpose and direction. For many in recovery, this step is a key part of not just avoiding alcohol or drugs, but also of living a life that's meaningful and fulfilling.

PASSING ON THE MESSAGE

Step12 - Having had a spiritual awakening as the result of these Steps, we tried to carry this message to alcoholics, and to practice these principles in all our affairs.

Step 12 is about sharing the journey and lessons of recovery with others who are still struggling with alcoholism. This step revolves around the idea that working through the AA steps leads to a significant personal transformation, often referred to as a "spiritual awakening." This isn't just about a spiritual awakening within the context of religious beliefs; it's a deep, personal shift in how we perceive ourselves, our addictions, and our interactions with the world. Writing this book has been a part of my mission to spread the powerful, transformative effects of the 12 steps—a journey I cherish deeply and am grateful to share.

In this step, we acknowledge the significant change in awareness and comprehension that completing the steps provides. It isn't only about understanding the nature of addiction; it's about gaining a broader insight into life, relationships, and self-discovery. The responsibility then extends to passing these insights on, whether through sponsoring newcomers, sharing our experiences in group meetings, or simply through everyday conversations. Writing about these experiences in various social media platforms and blogs can further spread the impactful message of recovery.

Step 12 encourages the application of honesty, humility, and spiritual growth in daily life, extending beyond recovery tactics to become principles for a more fulfilled and ethical existence. By aligning ourselves to these values in everyday actions and interactions, we demonstrate a living example not only to those struggling with addiction but also to the wider community. This practice helps maintain sobriety and improves overall life quality, as honesty in AA involves being truthful about our recovery journey, humility acknowledges the need for a supportive network, and spiritual growth fosters a connection beyond material life.

The impact of living these principles is deep, offering inspiration and a model for a sober, fulfilling life to others within the community. This continuous commitment to growth and service in Step 12 is more than a recovery conclusion, it invites a lifelong dedication to self-improvement and helping others. By consistently reflecting on and striving to better our actions, we not only ensure our recovery remains effective but also enrich our lives and those around us, reinforcing the transformative power of the AA program.

IT'S NOT ABOUT PERFECTION.

Many of us exclaimed "What an order I cannot go through with it "Don't be discouraged. No one among us has been able to maintain anything like perfect adherence to these principles. We are not saints. The point is that we are willing to grow along spiritual lines. The principles we have set down are guides to progress. We claim spiritual progress over spiritual perfection. AA Big Book page 60

The AA Big Book reaches out to those of us who might feel overwhelmed by the 12 Steps, acknowledging the daunting nature of this recovery path right from the start. It reassures us, "There's no way I can do all of this" is a common initial reaction, and the response is always, "Hey, don't worry about it." There's a universal understanding within AA that navigating these steps is challenging, and perfection isn't the expectation.

What truly matters is our willingness to grow and improve gradually. The 12 Steps serve as guiding principles rather than rigid rules that demand complete adherence. The core philosophy here is set out in the phrase, "We claim spiritual progress rather than spiritual perfection." This underscores the importance of continuous personal development over the unrealistic goal of perfect spirituality. It's about putting out effort, learning from our mistakes, and evolving over time. The essence of the journey lies in embracing our humanity—acknowledging that we are all fallible and imperfect—and focusing on personal growth at our own pace, offering ourselves grace instead of criticism for our imperfections.

CHAPTER 4 SUMMARY

Simplicity of AA:

The Alcoholics Anonymous 12-Step program focuses on simplicity in helping overcome addiction and facilitating a life overhaul.

Surrender:

The importance of admitting powerlessness over addiction as a foundational step to recovery, highlighting the strength that comes from acknowledging our vulnerabilities.

Accountability:

The necessity of facing our actions and their consequences through self-reflection and acknowledgment as a path towards genuine transformation.

Community Support:

The vital role of shared experiences and support from the AA community in overcoming the isolation of addiction.

The 12 Steps:

The AA program's steps, focusing on surrender to a higher power, self-examination, admitting wrongs, making amends, and continuous self-improvement.

Spiritual Growth:

Focus on spiritual growth and connection as key elements in recovery, beyond just abstaining from alcohol or drugs.

Daily Practice:

The importance of integrating the principles of the AA program into daily life for ongoing personal growth and recovery.

Helping Others:

The Twelve Steps encourages us who have made progress in our recovery journey to share our experiences and support others who are struggling with addiction.

Progress Over Perfection:

Reminds us that the goal is not to achieve perfection but to make continuous spiritual progress, accepting and learning from imperfections.

Main Points of Chapter Four:

By adopting the AA 12 step program's basic yet powerful principles, we can navigate the complexities of recovery and embrace a life of clarity, hope, and purpose. No matter how daunting the path to recovery may seem, through the steadfast support of a Twelve Step /AA community and a commitment to these guiding principles, a fulfilling and hopeful life is within reach.

CHAPTER 5

MIND BODY AND SOUL

As humans, we are intrinsically linked through a universal energy that integrates our mind, body, and soul. To achieve personal transformation and reach our highest potential, it's essential to find balance and nurture each aspect of ourselves. Modern science and medicine reveal how our thoughts, beliefs, emotions, and behaviors significantly influence our overall health and capacity for healing. Moreover, nature and the animal kingdom provide unique insights into holistic living, especially through our interactions with animals.

This leads me into exploring how animals, particularly our pets, offer heartfelt lessons on living a balanced life. My own experiences with dogs have not only deepened my connection to the natural world but have also enriched my understanding of recovery and personal growth. Dogs teach us about unconditional love, the importance of being present, and the joy of life's simplest pleasures. These lessons are especially valuable as they demonstrate how to harmonize our mental, physical, and emotional health. As we delve deeper into the insights gained from our furry friends, it becomes clear how these connections can positively impact our journey toward healing and well-being.

LESSONS FROM OUR FURRY FRIENDS.

I have always loved dogs. I was always drawn to their unconditional love, their innate way of just being. When I was growing up as a child, we had dogs. There was my grandparents dog Rex, who was a big old blind gentle soul. His eyes bright blue but cloudy from the cataracts. We were small kids running around my grandparent's big back garden in Finglas Dublin and he didn't mind all of the noise and the movement, he was just there with us.

And there was Major, he was my dog. I remember when we got him as a pup, I bonded with him straightway. I can still picture a summers day in our back garden. Major was just a puppy about nine weeks old. It was a hot day, one of those childhood summer days that we all remember. I had made a makeshift tent with a sofa throw in the garden, and I had taken Major under it for the shade, we both fell asleep on the grass, he was cuddled up to me. Later when he got bigger, he would head down to the row of shops on our road and wait for me to come home from school. It was like he had a built in timer he knew instinctively what time I would be coming home at, and he would sit there waiting patiently for me, then when he got sight of me his tail would wag and he would run up to me, I loved that feeling and I loved him. I remember the day that he died. Major had been knocked down by a car on our road. I was gutted, heartbroken. I guess as he got older his senses was not as sharp as they used to be. When I think back on that day it still hits me in the heart.

So I was about six months into my recovery when we decided as a family to get a dog. My daughter Caoimhe and I drove out to the animal shelter, Dogs Trust in Dublin, we were looking for a Staffie or a Pitbull Terrier. I have always believed that these breeds get a bad press. The public perception is not right and as a result they are misunderstood, I can identify with that. Anyway, after looking at a few different dogs the people in the shelter brought out Bella, straightway she came running to us. My daughter Caoimhe had hunched down, and Bella snuggled her head right under Caoimhe's arm pit and started licking her! That was it we were sold! We knew at once that she was the one. Just like Major all those years ago, I bonded with Bella straightway and along with my family she has played a big part in my Recovery. We may have rescued Bella, but she has rescued me also.

So, you may be asking what's the deal with the dog story. Well I believe we can learn a lot from our furry friends to help heal our mind body and soul in recovery! We can gain a great deal by spending time with a dog. I can definitely testify to that. Recovering from addiction is a tough journey with many ups and downs. For me having Bella by my side has made this journey a bit easier and more rewarding. It has had such a positive ripple effect on all of us in the family. I'll break it down so that I can demonstrate the benefits in a simple manner.

MIND

Being in the Now:

Dogs always live in the moment. They don't think about the past or future. This can teach us to focus on the present, which helps in controlling our thoughts and feeling less anxious. Remember our bodies are always in the present, just like a dogs, it's our minds that like to time travel. So align your mind with your body and be in the now.

Finding Happiness in Little Things:

Dogs get happy over simple stuff like walks or playing fetch. This shows us how to be happy with the small things in life, instead of relying on substances or big events. While I am writing this, I see Bella's face light up when I throw the ball for her and the joy, she gets from that, that brings me joy also.

Being Patient and Flexible:

Learning to understand and train a dog needs patience and the ability to adapt. These skills are really useful for someone recovering from addiction, as getting better takes time and involves facing different challenges. This training also benefits the dog as it keeps them mentally stimulated and keeps boredom at bay, something we need to be mindful of also. Patience and flexibility are skills that can be learned and with consistent practice we get better.

BODY

Staying Active and Healthy:

Dogs need activity and if you have a dog like Bella, she needs walking every day, and not just around the block! Walking and playing with a dog mean more physical activity, which is great for health. Exercise makes us and the dog feel good. Taking part in this gives us positive physical energy and can lessen the desire to use or pick up. I love walking in the park with Bella, it gets me out and keeps me fit.

Having a Routine:

Looking after a dog creates a regular schedule for things like feeding and walks. Dogs need feeding at the same time every day, As mentioned above, they need daily exercise and mental stimulation. Creating a routine and sticking to it nurtures a sense of discipline in us and helps in building a healthy and organised lifestyle.

Lowering Stress:

There is scientific evidence that spending time with a dog can lower our blood pressure and reduce stress. This is important for keeping our bodies healthy. Chilling out in the evening with Bella next to myself and my wife Mary is a very calming state of being.

SOUL

Feeling Loved and Accepted:

The love and acceptance a dog offers can be incredibly healing and comforting. Their love doesn't come with conditions; they don't care about your past mistakes; they simply love you for who you are. This kind of unconditional and pure love from a dog can teach us a lot about how to love and accept ourselves, just as we are. It also helps us learn to accept others without judging them based on their past or their flaws.

Connecting and Understanding Others:

Dogs have a way of helping us feel more connected to the world around us. They show us empathy in their way, responding to our emotions and offering comfort when we're down. Taking care of a dog, understanding their needs, and communicating with them can improve our ability to connect with and understand other people. It teaches us to pay attention to non-verbal cues, to be more patient, and to empathise with others' feelings and situations, which is a vital skill in building strong relationships.

Finding Purpose and Value:

Caring for a dog can gives us a strong sense of purpose and make us feel valued. It's about more than just feeding them or taking them for walks. It's knowing that our dog depends on us, trusts us, and loves us unconditionally. This responsibility can be incredibly empowering, especially for some of us in recovery who may be struggling to find our place or purpose in life. It provides a reason to get up in the morning and a sense of accomplishment that comes from caring for another living being.

Learning to Forgive:

One of the most remarkable things about dogs is their ability to forgive. They don't hold onto anger or resentment. If we step on our dog's tail by accident, they might yelp, but they won't stay mad at us. This ability to forgive and move on is something we can learn from dogs. It teaches us the power of forgiveness and compassion, not just towards others but also towards ourselves. Learning to let go of grudges and forgive can lead to a more peaceful and fulfilling life, which is especially important for all of us who working through the challenges of recovery. Let's sum this up simply. A dog can be a great companion for us in recovery. Dogs teach us important lessons about living in the moment, finding happiness in simple things, and loving unconditionally. These lessons can help heal our minds, keep our bodies active, and nourish our souls.

THE IMPORTANCE OF ENERGY

Hippocrates said, "The natural healing force within each one of us is the greatest force in getting well."

Quantum Physics supports this by showing that everything, including our thoughts, is made of energy. Our thoughts can influence our physical reality, and our hearts emit an electromagnetic field that affects every cell in our body, transmitting signals of health or distress. This energy field extends beyond our five senses and is part of a vast, universal network. In the quantum world, everything is energy, including our bodies and non-physical aspects like thoughts and emotions. Understanding this interconnectedness helps us see how changes in one area can impact our entire being. Different types of energy have various effects on our well-being, which we'll explore further.

Holistic well-being hinges on the interconnectedness of the mind, body, and soul, each influencing and supporting the others in a continuous interplay. Below we delve into the various types of energies that fuel these aspects, shedding light on how to nurture each to enhance overall health and vitality.

PHYSICAL ENERGY: FUELING THE BODY

Physical energy is the fundamental force that propels us through our daily activities, underpinning every action from the most mundane tasks to the most intense physical exertions. This type of energy is directly sourced from the essentials of life: the food we eat, the air we breathe, and the exercise we engage in. The caliber of these energy sources critically affects our overall health and stamina, making it paramount to select high-quality nutrients and maintain a consistent exercise regimen. Much like a high-performance sports car requires premium gasoline to operate optimally, our bodies need the best possible fuel—nutrient-rich foods, clean air, and regular physical activity—to function at their peak. Ensuring that our bodies receive top-tier nourishment involves more than just choosing the right foods; it encompasses a holistic approach to lifestyle choices that promote vigorous health. Integrating regular, varied physical activities into our routine not only enhances our physical energy but also boosts mental clarity and emotional well-being. These activities help circulate oxygen more efficiently, improving cellular function and resilience. By consciously choosing wholesome, unprocessed foods and committing to active living, we lay a strong foundation for sustained energy levels, robust health, and a vibrant life. This approach to managing our physical energy ensures that our body's systems are finely tuned, much like meticulously maintaining a high-performance engine, enabling us to meet life's demands with stamina and vitality.

MENTAL ENERGY: SHARPENING THE MIND

Mental energy is the generator that powers our cognitive functions, shaping our ability to think, learn, and solve problems. It's fueled by our thoughts and the intellectual activities we engage in daily. When we stimulate our minds with positive engagements—like learning new skills, engaging in challenging puzzles, or maintaining an optimistic outlook—our mental energy surges. This boost is akin to installing high-powered software in a supercomputer, which maximizes efficiency and output. Such positive mental activities ensure that our cognitive engines run smoothly, enhancing our capacity to process information swiftly and accurately. However, just as a supercomputer can be compromised by malware, our mental processes can be severely hindered by negative thoughts. Pessimism, worry, and mental stagnation act like viruses in our minds, slowing down thought processes and clouding clarity, resulting in mental fatigue and confusion.

To manage and enhance our mental energy effectively, it's crucial to cultivate a healthy mental environment. This involves surrounding ourselves with positive influences, seeking stimulating intellectual challenges, and practicing mindfulness to ward off the mental malware of negative thinking. By doing so, we not only preserve our cognitive health but also build a reservoir of mental energy that supports resilience and ongoing intellectual growth.

EMOTIONAL ENERGY: HARNESSING OUR FEELINGS

Emotional energy is a dynamic force that fuels our feelings and greatly influences our psychological landscape. It acts as a powerful stimulus, amplifying our emotional responses and shaping our thought patterns. When our emotional energy is high, our feelings and the thoughts they generate can become more intense, leading to vibrant, often overpowering cycles of emotion. This heightened state can elevate positive feelings like joy and excitement but can also exacerbate negative emotions such as anger or anxiety. Conversely, when emotional energy is low, our mood and mental activities may be subdued, leading to a state of lethargy or disengagement where both thoughts and emotions are muted.

Managing our emotional energy effectively requires a deep understanding of the continuous interaction between our thoughts and feelings. By fostering this awareness, we can develop greater emotional intelligence, which enables us to recognize and regulate our emotional states more skilfully. This process involves not only monitoring our emotions but also evaluating the thoughts that ignite and sustain these emotions. With practice, we can learn to influence our emotional energy positively, using it to foster resilience and emotional agility. This management allows us to navigate life's ups and downs with more grace and stability, ensuring that our emotional energy serves as a source of strength and adaptation rather than a trigger for instability.

SPIRITUAL ENERGY: CONNECTING WITH GREATER FORCES

Spiritual energy is a remarkable power that taps into our deepest sense of purpose and our connection to something beyond the individual self—be it a higher power, the universe, or the intricate beauty of the natural world. It's this energy that roots us to our core, offering a sense of grounding in a world that can often feel chaotic and disconnected. By engaging in practices such as meditation, prayer, and reflective contemplation, we can nurture and strengthen this spiritual connection, making it a reliable source of comfort and guidance. Maintaining a vibrant spiritual energy is not just beneficial, it's essential for leading a truly enriching life. It encourages us to live in harmony with our core values and beliefs, guiding our decisions and actions in a way that reflects our deepest convictions. This alignment infuses our daily lives with meaning and direction, helping us to navigate the challenges of life with a sense of purpose and resilience. As we cultivate our spiritual energy, we find that it not only enhances our own well-being but also empowers us to contribute positively to the world around us, creating a ripple effect of inspiration and upliftment.

SOCIAL ENERGY: THE POWER OF CONNECTIONS

Social energy is a powerful force derived from our interactions with others, playing a crucial role in shaping our mood and overall energy levels. Engaging positively with friends, family, and colleagues can be uplifting, significantly enhancing our mood and broadening our perspective on life. These interactions act as catalysts for positive emotional responses, boosting our spirits and providing a sense of connection and support. Conversely, negative interactions can have the opposite effect, draining our energy and leaving us feeling depleted and stressed. It's crucial to recognize the profound impact that the quality of our social engagements can have on our mental and emotional health. Effectively managing social energy requires intentional efforts to cultivate relationships that enrich our lives and shield us from those that sap our vitality. This involves nurturing connections with individuals who uplift and understand us, creating an environment of mutual support and positivity. Setting clear boundaries with those who drain our energy is equally important. By doing so, we protect our well-being and maintain our focus on building and sustaining nourishing interactions. Establishing these boundaries not only preserves our energy but also empowers us to invest more deeply in relationships that are truly fulfilling and aligned with our needs and values, ensuring that our social life enhances, rather than detracts from, our overall quality of life.

THE ENERGY OF FAITH

The Energy of Faith is a critical yet often overlooked component of our holistic well-being, intertwining deeply with the social, spiritual, emotional, and mental energies that vitalize our lives. This dynamic energy extends beyond traditional religious contexts to include the faith we hold in ourselves, a higher power, and our communal bonds. It provides a sense of direction and comfort, acting as a compass through life's uncertainties and supporting our resilience against challenges. By believing in something greater than ourselves, we gain spiritual relief and a peaceful acceptance that cushions the emotional and psychological impacts of our struggles, reinforcing our capacity to handle life's hardships with grace. At a personal level, the Energy of Faith fosters self-confidence and a resilient mindset, crucial for personal growth and overcoming obstacles. It enhances our belief in our own abilities and underpins the decisions that reflect our true values. Socially, it strengthens the connections within our community, providing emotional support and practical help that are vital for navigating life's ups and downs. Engaging in practices that reinforce this faith—such as meditation, prayer, writing affirmations, or participating in support groups—can deepen our connections and fortify our spiritual resilience. Embracing the Energy of Faith empowers us to lead lives filled with hope, strength, and a profound sense of community, aligning our actions with our deepest values for a fulfilling and balanced existence.

FUSION: THE SYMPHONY OF ENERGIES

Understanding the interconnectedness of different energies within us is necessary for achieving holistic well-being. Recognizing this connection simplifies our approach to health and wellness. When we see how all of these energies are intertwined, it becomes clearer how changes in one area can positively affect the others and allow us to strike a balance more effectively. All of these energies converge within and around us to make up the whole of the human spirit. This interconnectedness extends to the greater energy of the universe, suggesting that we are all part of a larger, unified whole. Experiencing abundance, harmony, and love becomes more accessible when we view ourselves as part of this unified field. Abundance is not just a physical state; it's a mindset that recognizes the richness of our existence in all aspects. When we align our energies and live in a state of balance, we open ourselves to the abundance of experiences, relationships, and opportunities that life offers. Harmony is achieved when all of our energies are in sync and as one. This harmonious state is crucial for experiencing love – love for ourselves, for others, and for the world. By fostering this harmony, we cultivate a loving approach towards life and relationships, enriching our experiences and interactions.

The simplicity in this holistic approach lies in understanding that we don't need to silo or separately manage different aspects of our being. Instead, by nurturing one area, we can positively influence others. This simplifies our approach to life and well-being. It allows us to move gracefully and naturally in nurturing our energies, leading to a life that is not just balanced but also deeply connected with the essence of the human spirit and the greater energy of our higher power.

By embracing this interconnectedness, we can bring simplicity into the very fabric of our life. We start to see ourselves and our place in the world differently – not as isolated individuals but as vital parts of a greater whole. This shift in attitude can lead to a great sense of fulfilment, peace, and a deep, abiding connection with the universal flow of energy.

CHAPTER FIVE SUMMARY

Lessons from Furry Friends:

The similarities between companionship with dogs and recovery, drawing on the therapeutic benefits of living in the moment and unconditional love.

A Holistic Approach:

We must come to our recovery holistically, focusing on the connection between mind, body, and soul.

The Influence of Energy:

Everything including our thoughts and emotions, is energy, impacting our physical health and recovery.

Quantum Physics Insight:

Everything of us and around us is energy. Our thoughts can impact our physical well-being. Encourage positive thinking as a way to promote healing. The connection between our mindset and our body's health is very real.

Physical Energy:

Importance of nutrition, exercise, and proper breathing in maintaining health and stamina.

Mental Energy:

Partaking in stimulating activities and positive outlook boosts our cognitive function and emotional well-being.

Emotional Energy:

Our emotional energy impacts our mood and overall energy, focus on healthy emotional expression and coping strategies.

Spiritual Energy:

Learn to practice meditation and align our actions with our personal values for a fulfilling recovery journey.

Social Energy:

Encourage fostering positive connections and setting boundaries with toxic relationships to enhance well-being.

Faith and Energy:

The chapter underscores the 'Energy of Faith,' which includes faith in a higher power, oneself, and the supportive community, playing a transformative role in recovery.

Interconnectedness of Energies:

The collective influence of different energy types on our holistic well-being promotes a balanced recovery approach.

Main Points of Chapter Five:

Recovery is a holistic process that integrates mind, body, and soul, emphasising the vital role of balancing various energies for overall well-being. By focusing on positive thinking, engaging in physical activities, expressing emotions healthily, and nurturing our spiritual and social connections, we can significantly enhance our journey towards a fulfilling life.

CHAPTER 6

RELATIONSHIPS AND COMMUNITY

In our recovery journey, the influence of relationships and community cannot be overstated. This chapter delves deeper into the essential role that social connections play in supporting and sustaining our recovery efforts. From the supportive bonds formed in family settings to the solidarity found within recovery groups, our interactions provide a vital network of support that echoes the significance of community discussed in previous chapters. Relationships rooted in empathy and understanding offer a sanctuary for open expression, allowing us to share our struggles and triumphs. Such connections do more than offer comfort; they actively propel us forward on our path to sobriety. The sense of belonging we gain from being part of a community that comprehends the nuances of addiction bolsters our resolve and enriches our recovery process. It's within these supportive networks that we find not only a reflection of our own experiences but also the collective strength to persevere.

Furthermore, the structured environment of support groups and 12-step programs provides more than companionship; they foster a setting where vulnerability is not just encouraged but essential. The shared wisdom and coping strategies gleaned from these groups equip us with practical tools to navigate the complexities of sobriety. Recognizing our journey as part of a broader narrative of resilience and renewal can be incredibly empowering, illuminating the path ahead with hope and possibility.

The impact of nurturing relationships extends into promoting healthy lifestyle changes. The encouragement to adopt better habits and pursue new interests, underpinned by a community's support, can significantly enhance our well-being. This dynamic of mutual support not only aids in our personal transformation but also showcases the profound effect of positive connections in recovery. Through these relationships, we begin to see the world anew and reconnect in meaningful ways, thus reinforcing the transformative power of community.

Just as a garden thrives with proper care and the right conditions, so too does our recovery flourish with the nourishment of understanding and shared experiences. These relationships are the sunlight and water that encourage growth, resilience, and a reaffirmed belief in our potential. By cultivating and valuing these connections, we not only rebuild our lives but also foster a thriving, supportive network that upholds our continued sobriety and personal growth.

SIMPLE AND AUTHENTIC CONNECTIONS

In recovery, building simple, authentic connections is like laying down a solid foundation for a house—essential for stability and resilience. These genuine relationships provide a safe environment where we can share our experiences, strengths, and hopes without fear of judgment. Authentic connections often lead to the discovery of a shared journey, where similarities of experience overshadow differences.

Let's consider Rachel's story. Before discovering the supportive embrace of a recovery community, Rachel's life was a solitary journey marked by quiet struggles and unspoken challenges. Isolated in her experiences, she navigated a world that seemed devoid of genuine connections, where understanding and empathy were scarce commodities. Her days were colored by the weight of a hidden battle, one she fought silently behind a facade of normalcy. This loneliness not only exacerbated her struggles but also deepened her sense of detachment from the world around her. The turning point came when Rachel, driven by a mix of desperation and hope, decided to step out of her isolation. She chose to attend a local support group, a decision fraught with anxiety yet tinged with the promise of change. It was here, in the humble setting of a community center filled with others who shared similar paths, that Rachel would take her first steps toward true healing.

This environment, unfamiliar yet strangely comforting, offered her the first real opportunity to connect with others who understood the depth of her struggles without needing her to explain. Surrounded by people who had faced similar battles, she found a space where she could openly share her deepest fears, moments of failure, and small victories without fear of being judged or misunderstood. This act of sharing, something she had avoided for so long, became a crucial step in her recovery. The safety she felt while baring her vulnerability to the group was healing, building courage, commitment, and connection to her soul. As she listened to others and saw nods of understanding and empathy, Rachel realized she wasn't alone. Her unique story shared common threads with the stories of those around her. Each meeting, each conversation, added another layer to Rachel's sense of belonging. Her experiences, once a source of shame and isolation, became the very things that connected her to this new community.

This sense of belonging fuelled Rachel's healing process. She found strength in the group's honesty and openness, encouraging her to keep going, even on the toughest days. The support group became more than just a place to share; it was a source of constant encouragement, a reminder of her progress, and proof of the transformative power of finding a community where honesty and openness are not just valued but foundational.

NAVIGATING RELATIONSHIPS IN RECOVERY

Focusing on the benefits of relationships and community is essential, but it's also crucial to recognize the drag that negative relationships from our past can have on our energy, resilience, and progress. Relationships rooted in past substance abuse can pull us back into cycles we're desperate to break free from. These connections, often built on unstable foundations, can reintroduce temptation and trigger relapse. Likewise, people who normalize or even glorify substance abuse can dissolve our resolve, making it harder to maintain sobriety.

This challenge requires us to identify which relationships and community ties nourish our recovery and which ones threaten it. It's about setting boundaries that protect our sobriety and actively choosing to spend time with those who respect and support our journey. Let's explore Terry's story. Before embarking on his journey to sobriety, Terry's life was a tragic roundabout of fleeting highs and prolonged lows, dominated by a lifestyle that revolved around alcohol and drug use. He was a familiar face in many circles where nights blurred into mornings without pause, and relationships were often transient and superficial. These connections, while plentiful, were shallow roots in unstable soil, offering little in the way of true support or stability. Terry's days were marked by a persistent feeling of running in place, never quite advancing toward any meaningful goal or fulfillment.

Living in a close knit district where everyone knew each other's business, Terry often felt the weight of public scrutiny, which only fueled his inner turmoil and dependency. His identity had become intertwined with his habits, defining how others saw him and, crucially, how he viewed himself. It was a life characterized by dependency and denial, shadowed by the knowledge that each passing day drifted further away from what he once hoped he might become. This backdrop of internal conflict and external expectations set the stage for Terry's profound realization of the need for change, prompting his courageous step towards recovery and a complete transformation of his social landscape. In the early days of his sobriety, Terry found himself torn between the comfort of familiar faces and the realization that these old connections, steeped in substance use, posed a significant threat to his newfound stability. Each interaction with the past was a tug-of-war, with nostalgia and habit on one side and his deep-seated desire for change on the other. Realizing the risky nature of his situation, Terry made a conscious decision to redefine his social territory.

This wasn't an easy journey. It required Terry to critically evaluate each relationship, weighing its impact on his sobriety. By cutting away unhealthy connections, he made room for new, nourishing relationships to flourish. Terry sought out support groups and recovery communities, spaces where vulnerability was seen as a strength. In these circles, he found others who understood the language of loss and redemption, and who were committed to building a life beyond addiction. But Terry's transformation went beyond avoiding negative influences; it was about actively cultivating positive ones. He learned the value of relationships built on mutual respect, shared growth, and unconditional support. These connections became the bedrock of his recovery, offering not just a safety net for tough times but also a source of joy and fulfilment. As Terry's social circle evolved, so did his sense of self, no longer defined by addiction but as someone capable of change, growth, and resilience.

BLOCKERS AND UNLOCKERS

In recovery, we encounter people who either drain us of energy or fill us with it. Those who drain us are the "Blockers," often plugging their negative energy into us, making it harder to maintain hope and positivity. These individuals might not even realize the impact they have, but their influence can cast a long shadow over our efforts to stay sober. Navigating relationships with Blockers, especially when they're close to us, is particularly tough. Whether it's a partner, parent, sibling, or friend, their negative outlook or disbelief in our recovery process can feel like a personal attack. It's a delicate balance, wanting to keep them in our lives but also needing to protect our sobriety. Dealing with these situations requires honesty, boundaries, and sometimes tough decisions. Conversely, there are people who naturally lift our spirits—the "Unlockers." These individuals exude a warm, positive energy that draws people toward them almost magnetically. They possess a genuine spirit of kindness and compassion, making us feel seen, heard, valued, and understood. In their presence, our worries fade away, replaced by a sense of calm and reassurance. Without even trying, they unlock a sense inside us that goodness and light exist in the world.

TIPS FOR NURTURING HEALTHY RELATIONSHIPS

Nurturing healthy relationships in recovery is like tending a garden—it requires patience, care, and the right environment to flourish. Here are eight practical tips on how to cultivate such relationships:

1. Communicate Openly:

Be honest about your feelings, experiences, and needs. Open communication builds trust and helps others understand your journey better.

2. Set Clear Boundaries:

Protect your sobriety by clearly articulating your limits, such as not wanting to be around substances or needing time for meetings and self-care.

3. Seek Supportive Environments:

Surround yourself with people who respect and support your recovery journey, such as friends from support groups or understanding loved ones.

4. Give Back:

Strengthen relationships by being supportive yourself. Offer a listening ear, share your experiences, and help others in their time of need.

5. Pursue Shared Interests:

Build relationships around activities that don't involve substances. Shared interests provide a solid foundation for healthy connections.

6. Practice Forgiveness:

Let go of past hurts to open the door to more fulfilling relationships. Forgiveness is key to healing and growth.

7. Invest Time and Effort:

Relationships thrive on mutual effort and care. Spend quality time with loved ones and show appreciation for their support.

8. Stay Positive:

Focus on the good in people and situations. A positive outlook can attract like-minded individuals and strengthen your support network.

By following these tips, you can nurture healthy relationships that support your recovery, offering both strength and joy on your journey. Remember, we're seeking progress, not perfection. Healthy relationships help us "Keep The Faith" in our recovery journey. Nurturing healthy relationships in recovery is like tending a garden—it requires patience, care, and the right environment to flourish.

As we navigate the complex paths of recovery, it becomes very clear that our progress is not measured solely by individual milestones, but by the connections we forge along the way. Relationships and community are not mere backdrops to our journey; they are integral to the very essence of our healing. In every shared story, every word of encouragement, and every moment of mutual vulnerability, we find the strength to persevere and the courage to redefine our lives.

Embracing this communal tapestry, we recognize that recovery is a collective endeavor—an interwoven blend of personal effort and communal support. As we close this chapter, let us carry forward the undeniable truth that we are stronger together. In the symphony of shared struggles and successes, we find a vibrant chorus that uplifts and sustains us. Here, in the heart of our communities, lies the potent force for lasting change, propelling us not just toward recovery, but toward a life rich with connection and purpose. Let us commit to nurturing these bonds, for they are the very soul of our journey to sobriety and beyond.

CHAPTER SIX SUMMARY

Importance of connection:

Family, friends, and community are crucial in recovery, offering support through both hard and happy times.

Positive Influences:

Positive people around us can encourage healthier choices and help us grow.

Power of Empathy and Shared Experience:

Sharing experiences and receiving empathy from others gives us a safe place to be ourselves, making the recovery journey less lonely.

Role of Support Groups:

Support groups and 12-step programs offer invaluable guidance and a structured environment for healing.

Healthy Lifestyle Changes:

Being around supportive people motivates us to live healthier and pursue new hobbies or interests that support our sobriety.

Simple, Authentic Connections:

Building simple, honest relationships is key, like finding a sense of belonging in a support group, which can be a vital part of healing.

Reconnecting with Purpose:

Recovery lets us rediscover old passions or find new activities that fill the void left by addiction with purpose and satisfaction.

Nurturing Positive Relationships:

To maintain and grow healthy relationships in recovery, it's important to communicate openly, set boundaries, find supportive groups, help others, share interests, practice forgiveness, invest time and effort, and stay positive.

Main Points Chapter Six:

Family, friends and community support play a crucial part of sustained recovery. Positive influences and shared experiences can significantly aid the healing process. We seek to develop healthy lifestyle changes and the pursuit of passions as a means of filling the void left by addiction. The reconnection with purpose to foster satisfaction and fulfilment in life.

NAVIGATING CHALLENGES

I magine you're on the brink of a significant life change, feeling a mix of nervousness and excitement. You're ready to leave behind old habits and step into a world full of potential. Close your eyes, take a deep breath, and picture yourself at the start of this new journey. Feel the anticipation in your chest, hear the sounds around you, and see the path ahead. How does this moment make you feel?

As I ventured into the unknown, doubts and fears occasionally clouded my vision, whispering tales of potential failure and relapse. Yet, it was this very fear that forged my resolve, fueling my journey with a newfound faith. With each step forward, the fresh air of possibility filled my lungs, and though the path was riddled with potential setbacks, my direction was propelled by an internal compass of hope. I was not just fleeing a past polluted by addiction; I was moving towards a richer, more authentic life. Though my course wasn't clear, my faith assured me that my direction was right. There was only Plan A, simple. In Plan A, the air felt fresh, full of new chances. Taking that first step, I knew it wouldn't be easy. There would be hard times and obstacles. But at that moment of commencement, I felt hopeful. I was drawn to this new path, ready for the challenges and opportunities it would bring. As I left my past behind and looked to the future, I felt optimistic. The unknown, though intimidating, seemed like a place full of possibilities. I was on this journey not just to escape my past but to find a new, better way of living. It was going to be challenging, but the prospect of discovering who I could become and living a life true to myself was thrilling. This was more than just a fresh start; it was my chance to truly free myself and live fully.

THE CHALLENGES

Recovery is inherently a voyage over rugged terrain—marked by peaks of triumph and valleys of despair. As someone on this road, I want to speak openly about the challenges that come with it. It's not just about abstinence. It's about confronting life head-on, shedding the crutches of past addictions to face the raw realities of existence. This journey, while rewarding, is far from easy. Each challenge, from emotional turbulence to social pressures, tests our resilience and fortitude. Yet, it is within these trials that the true strength of the human spirit is refined. By keeping it simple, we can navigate these challenges with grace and resilience. The road to recovery is full of challenges that require more than mere willpower to overcome. Emotional turbulence can shake our core, while social pressures to revert to old habits threaten our progress. Each test we face is a lesson in resilience, pushing us to develop a deeper understanding of ourselves and our capacities. By approaching these challenges with simplicity and maintaining focus on the present, we can navigate through them with greater ease and grace.

Navigating the challenges of recovery requires us to face a variety of difficult moments, each demanding its own unique approach and resilience. From the deep introspection needed to wrestle with our past, through the delicate balance required to manage emotional turmoil, to the vigilance needed to handle social pressures and triggers, each aspect of recovery is a critical piece of the larger journey. As we move forward, let's explore each of these challenges in detail, understanding how they shape our path to recovery and how embracing simplicity and focusing on the present can help us tackle them with greater clarity and strength. This exploration is not just about identifying the hurdles but learning how to transform these challenges into opportunities for profound personal growth and a renewed sense of purpose.

FACING OUR PAST

Wrestling with our past is like navigating a turbulent sea. Each memory of past mistakes can threaten to drag us under if we allow it. However, steering through this storm involves more than sheer willpower; it requires an honest examination of our actions and the courage to seek forgiveness—not only from others but from ourselves. This reconciliation with our past is not about erasing it but learning to dance with the waves of remorse and using these lessons as beacons for future growth. In confronting our history, we must harness the strength to face each wave of guilt and regret head-on. It's about acknowledging the harm we've caused and making amends where possible, which can be a deeply humbling and transformative process. This isn't merely about seeking redemption from those we've wronged; it's about fundamentally changing our relationship with ourselves. By forgiving ourselves, we set a course for a future that honors our growth and the sincere efforts we've made to improve. Through this process, our past misdeeds, rather than anchoring us in shame, become powerful lessons that propel us forward, guiding our journey towards a more conscious and fulfilling life.

EMOTIONAL TURMOIL

Emotions serve an important function – they help us to know what protects or threatens our survival and wellbeing. While physical sensations give us information about our physical wellbeing, emotional sensations do the same. The information we receive through our emotions is as important for us to notice as other physiological information, such as hunger and thirst. Otherwise, the urge to release the repressed emotional sensation will escalate to the point it will be impossible to manage. This uncontrollable emotional release is damaging to our reputation, self-confidence, and wellbeing.

Emotions, much like the primary colors of an artist's palette, are universally innate and shared by all of us. There are no emotions exclusively yours; they are a fundamental part of the human experience. We all feel them packaged neatly within our human nature. Just as an artist begins with primary colors that can't be created by mixing others, our primary emotions form the base of our emotional spectrum. From these, a myriad of feelings emerge through different combinations and intensities. Some emotions strike with overwhelming intensity, making us feel as though we're on the verge of overflowing, while others are so gentle they're almost imperceptible. Emotions can be mapped along two main dimensions: affect and arousal. Affect measures how pleasant or unpleasant an emotion is, spanning a spectrum from deeply unpleasant to highly pleasant. Picture this like the spectrum of light, ranging from the dark, cool hues of blues and purples to the bright, warm tones of reds and yellows, with many shades in between that subtly affect our mood and perception.

The second aspect, arousal, gauges the intensity of our physical response to emotions, from calming to agitating effects. For instance, while sadness might tug at us with an undesirable affect, it typically induces a lower state of arousal, sparing us severe physiological reactions. In contrast, anger is a high-arousal emotion, often gearing us up into a state of heightened physical readiness, with symptoms like a racing heart or sweaty palms.

Understanding these aspects is more than a theoretical exercise—it's a practical tool for life. By learning and practicing emotional regulation techniques, we can shift from merely reacting to our emotions in the heat of the moment to thoughtfully responding to them. This mastery over our responses allows us to navigate life's complexities with greater ease and stability. Emotional balance is a crucial skill in recovery from addiction, helping individuals manage intense emotions without reverting to substance use. Here are eight effective tools and techniques that can aid in this process:

1. Mindfulness Meditation:

Engaging in mindfulness meditation is like setting a compass for the mind. It teaches us to remain anchored in the 'now,' helping to clear the mental clutter that can lead to stress and relapse. By regularly practicing mindfulness, individuals in recovery can enhance their ability to observe their thoughts and emotions without getting swept away by them. This practice fosters a deepened sense of peace and stability, essential for navigating the day-to-day challenges of recovery.

2. Cognitive Behavioral Therapy (CBT):

Cognitive Behavioural Therapy is like refining our navigational charts; it helps pinpoint and correct the cognitive distortions that often lead to addictive behaviors. CBT equips us with a toolkit to challenge and change destructive thoughts, thereby transforming how they respond to various triggers. This process is crucial for recovery as it builds resilience against the pressures that might otherwise compel us back to substance use. Over time, CBT can fundamentally alter the way we approaches life's challenges, promoting healthier decision-making and problem-solving skills.

3. Deep Breathing Exercises:

Techniques such as diaphragmatic breathing are akin to finding a calm port in a storm. These exercises directly counteract the body's stress response, promoting relaxation and reducing the physical symptoms of anxiety—like rapid heartbeat and shallow breathing. With practice, deep breathing becomes a quick and effective tool for managing acute stress and anxiety, providing a momentary pause that allows for more thoughtful responses rather than reactive decisions.

4. Journaling:

Journaling is like keeping a Captain's Log on a long voyage. It allows for reflection and analysis of thoughts and emotions, providing insights that might not be evident in the moment. This practice can be particularly therapeutic, as it helps us process and release emotions constructively, avoiding the buildup of internal stress which can lead to relapse. Furthermore, looking back over previous entries can offer encouragement, showing how far we has come in their recovery journey.

5. Exercise:

Physical activity releases endorphins, improves mood, and reduces stress, helping to manage emotions more effectively. My journey has taught me the value of physical exercise as a potent tool for emotional regulation, echoing Gerry Hussey's insights in his book Awaken Your Power Within on the cleansing power of movement.

6. Support Groups:

Participating in support groups is like tending to a community garden where everyone brings their own experiences and wisdom to nurture growth. Each member contributes to the collective health of the garden, sharing nutrients in the form of support, advice, and understanding. This shared cultivation reinforces that no one needs to nurture their recovery alone. The encouragement and camaraderie found in these groups act like sunlight and water, essential for growth, boosting our motivation and strengthening our resolve through the seasons of recovery.

7. Scheduled Daily Activities:

Carefully structuring our day with a balance of work, relaxation, and social interaction is akin to maintaining a well-kept garden. Just as a gardener establishes routines to keep the garden flourishing—watering, weeding, and planting according to a schedule—creating a stable routine prevents the weeds of emotional turmoil from taking root. This daily structure ensures every part of our life is tended to, supporting both our recovery and overall well-being. Engaging regularly with others and allowing time for leisure are like enriching the soil, enhancing our emotional resilience and enabling us to weather the storms and droughts of recovery with greater ease.

8. Developing Patience:

Patience is a cornerstone of recovery, especially when it comes to navigating our emotions. Just like a gardener tending to new seeds, we must give ourselves the grace to heal at our own pace. Emotional stability isn't rebuilt in a day; it unfolds slowly, like seeds sprouting in fertile soil. As we nurture these seeds with patience and care, they gradually take root, growing stronger and more resilient over time. During this period of regeneration, the company of understanding friends and family who can offer a steadying hand and words of encouragement are invaluable. Remember to practice self-compassion. This kindness to oneself is a beacon of light that not only illuminates our inner darkness but also drives away the shadows of turmoil, replacing them with warmth and love.

Ultimately, navigating emotional turmoil is about finding strength in vulnerability. It requires us to be honest about our feelings and experiences and to seek help when needed. This journey, though filled with challenges, leads to deep personal growth and a better understanding of ourselves. As we learn to manage these emotions, the fog begins to lift, revealing a clearer path to a future defined by hope, resilience, and inner peace. As we master the art of emotional balance, the mists of uncertainty begin to clear. What emerges is a vision of our future, brightly outlined with hope, fortified by resilience, and serene with the promise of inner peace. This journey is not just about overcoming; it's about discovering a more powerful sense of self and moving confidently towards a life marked by emotional well-being.

SOCIAL PRESSURES AND TRIGGERS

Navigating the hazardous terrain of social pressures and triggers in recovery can be like walking through a minefield. Each step must be taken with caution, as the lure of old habits and the temptation of "just one more time" pose constant threats. These triggers are not merely external temptations; they represent deep-seated tests of our resolve to maintain a new way of life. From the familiar sight of a favorite bar to the scent of cigarette smoke or the sound of a song that once accompanied nights of excess, these cues can unexpectedly arouse powerful memories, pulling us towards our old ways. This battle is not just about resisting a substance; it's a serious challenge to resist reverting to a life that nearly destroyed us.

The difficulty intensifies when people from our past, who remain untouched by the transformations we have undergone, invite us back into high-risk environments. These are not just social invitations but pivotal moments that test our commitment to recovery. Rejecting these invitations requires more than a polite "no." It demands a strength and determination rooted deeply in our commitment to stay sober. To navigate these treacherous waters successfully, we must arm ourselves with strategies to swiftly exit risky situations. This includes proactively identifying potential triggers, having an escape plan for high-risk scenarios, and building a supportive network that understands the stakes involved in our journey toward sustained sobriety.

Moreover, effectively managing social pressures extends beyond just avoiding temptations; it involves actively creating and enforcing boundaries that safeguard our sobriety. Deciding who stays in our life and what settings we deem safe are critical choices that shape our recovery landscape. For many, this may mean severing ties with certain individuals or steering clear of specific places that jeopardize our sobriety. This proactive approach ensures that our environment supports our recovery goals, aligning with our new path toward a healthier, more fulfilling future. It's about saying yes to a life worth living and making deliberate choices that reinforce our commitment to health, happiness, and authenticity. Each decision in the face of these pressures represents a crucial step toward or away from the life we aspire to lead, emphasizing the importance of vigilance and wise decision-making in maintaining our trajectory toward recovery.

BUILDING NEW RELATIONSHIPS

In recovery, fostering new relationships means connecting with people who support the life we're actively choosing to lead. Gone are the days when our connections might have centered around shared habits of drinking or using. Now, our relationships are founded on honesty, respect, and mutual growth. Picture sitting down with someone to discuss your goals, fears, and the steps you're taking towards a better life, all without facing judgment or expectations rooted in your past. This transition into forming new bonds is both exhilarating and daunting. It involves venturing into unknown territory, where we openly share our challenges and triumphs. This openness can feel vulnerable and raw, yet it's incredibly genuine. These new relationships become pivotal, offering us a safety net on difficult days and acting as our cheerleaders when we triumph. This level of openness and honesty isn't easy, especially with a past colored by alcoholism and addiction where secrecy and deceit often prevailed. It's akin to walking into a room full of strangers and realizing you have the opportunity to co-create new narratives. These stories aren't tethered to past habits of drinking and drug use but are rich with possibilities for personal growth. Every conversation and shared moment lays another brick in the foundation of your new life. We come to rely on these individuals not as a means of escaping reality but as sources of strength and encouragement to confront it head-on.

Cultivating these new connections requires us to be transparent about our past and our aspirations for the future. It demands showing up, even when it's challenging, and letting others see our true selves. It's about shedding the mask and embracing authenticity. In return, we gain the opportunity to see them truly, to grow alongside them, and to build relationships founded not on a past of substance use but, on a hopeful, healing future. This is the core of recovery: linking arms with others who understand the journey and stepping forward together towards a brighter, healthier tomorrow.

REBUILDING TRUST

When mistrust clouds our perspective, it warps the way we see and interact with the world, hindering our ability to cultivate a positive reality. This state of skepticism prompts us to approach life with an exploitative mindset rather than one of curiosity and openness. Mistrust breeds fear, leading us to attempt control or destruction of the very things we fear. As a result, our efforts to create and contribute can become futile, often spiraling into pain and destruction. This destructive cycle not only harms the world around us but also threatens our own wellbeing. Without a foundation of trust and love, our every attempt to build or grow is undermined, and all our efforts may unwittingly contribute to a cycle of negativity and destruction.

To reverse this trend and foster a brighter, more hopeful future, cultivating trust is essential. Trust acts as a solvent to fear, allowing us to open up to new possibilities and engage with the world in a meaningful and constructive manner. When we trust, we allow ourselves to explore rather than exploit, to connect rather than contain. This shift in perspective enables us to participate in the loving union of life's experiences, creating a reality filled with positivity and purpose. Embracing trust means dismantling the barriers we have built around ourselves, preventing us from damaging both the world and our place within it. Only through trust can we stop the cycle of fear and destruction and start to build a beautiful new reality. In recovery, forging new relationships is a decisive step towards building a life that mirrors our renewed aspirations. These relationships, unlike those of our past that may have been cemented by shared habits of drinking or using, are founded on principles of honesty, respect, and a mutual commitment to personal growth. Picture yourself sitting across from someone, sharing your aspirations and fears openly, discussing the steps you are taking towards a healthier life—all without the fear of judgment or the weight of past mistakes clouding the interaction.

This journey into new relational territories can be exhilarating yet intimidating. We are charting unknown waters, revealing our vulnerabilities, and celebrating our victories in ways that are profoundly sincere. These fresh bonds form a crucial support network: they are our safety net on challenging days and our cheerleaders during triumphs. However, this requires a level of openness and truthfulness that might feel daunting after years shrouded in the shadows of addiction and deceit—where hiding and dishonesty were once survival mechanisms. As we step into new social circles, it feels as if we are entering a room full of strangers with the unique opportunity to co-author new narratives. These narratives are void of substance abuse, rich in opportunities for growth and self-discovery. Each interaction, each shared moment, lays another brick in the foundation of our new lives. We come to rely on these individuals not as an escape from reality but as pillars of strength and encouragement, helping us face the world as it is.

Engaging in these relationships means being transparent about our past and our hopes for the future. It demands that we show up authentically, ready to let go of our masks and engage genuinely. In doing so, we not only see others more clearly but also engage in mutual growth, forging bonds based on a hopeful, healthy outlook rather than a shared history of addiction. This is the crux of recovery: building connections, based on trust, with those who comprehend the depth of the journey and walking alongside them towards a brighter, more fulfilling future.

STAYING COMMITTED TO RECOVERY.

This is a daily dedication to living sober. Every single day will present its own set of challenges. We face the task of handling cravings, sticking to healthy habits, and always looking for ways to grow personally. Consistency is the key here to this journey, keeping things simple and staying focused on the present are our strongest assets. Every day in recovery is a precious opportunity to write a new chapter in our ongoing story of renewal. Each morning brings with it a fresh slate of decisions that can either bolster our resolve to remain sober or pose tests to our commitment. It is vital that we cultivate a keen sense of self-awareness, delve into understanding how our minds operate, and engage in sincere self-reflection. Managing cravings extends beyond mere resistance against old habits. It involves a deeper comprehension of the triggers that spark these urges. This understanding empowers us to develop more effective strategies to handle stress, alleviate boredom, and soothe emotional distress. By learning to identify and cope with these triggers, we equip ourselves with the tools necessary for sustained recovery and a balanced, fulfilling life. Establishing and upholding healthy routines forms the bedrock of our dedication to recovery. This commitment often manifests through regular exercise, balanced nutrition, and sufficient rest, but recovery transcends physical health alone. Embracing a holistic approach is essential for enduring sobriety. Engaging in activities that enrich the soul—whether it's through creative endeavors, enjoying nature, or nurturing relationships with loved ones—strengthens our resolve to maintain a sober life daily.

These routines provide more than mere structure; they fortify our resilience, preparing us to navigate life's inevitable challenges without reverting to substance use. By consistently investing in these practices, we not only support our physical well-being but also cultivate a deeper, more sustainable form of recovery that permeates every aspect of our lives.

Throughout this book, I've repeatedly emphasized the importance of personal development. It's about being constantly open to new lessons and insights that reinforce our recovery journey. This might involve drawing wisdom from the shared experiences in support groups, discovering hobbies that spark joy and fulfillment, or dedicating moments for self-reflection to assess our progress and set future objectives. Engaging in these activities encourages continuous personal growth, ensuring that our recovery is not only maintained but also enriched and deepened over time. By embracing simplicity and anchoring ourselves in the present, we shield against the overwhelm that can come from the "what ifs" looming in our futures or the shadows of past regrets. It's about approaching recovery one day at a time, celebrating each small victory, and acknowledging every bit of progress, no matter its size. This daily commitment to recovery exceeds mere abstinence; it's about crafting a life where sobriety is woven into the fabric of a fuller, more meaningful existence. Each day is a step toward not just staying sober, but living a life enriched by new experiences and deeper connections.

FINDING PURPOSE

Lastly, recovery challenges us to find new meaning and purpose in our lives. I will spend a little time here with you as I believe that finding purpose in our life is a truly wonderful experience. It is also a transformative experience. I say transformative as it's not just change. Change is a process, transformation happens within us. Change holds the possibility of reverting back whereas transformation alters us in a permanent way. When a caterpillar transforms to a butterfly it cannot go back to being a caterpillar. When we transform, we go beyond change, beyond simply leaving drink and drugs behind. We look deeply and searchingly into who we are, what we love, and how we want to impact the world. This introspection is both challenging and exhilarating, as it asks us to open ourselves up to new possibilities and to our inner potential. It challenges us to redefine our understanding of fulfilment and success. It is the feed for our internal need.

Moving beyond addiction opens a door to a world where we can align our daily actions with what truly matters to us. This could mean rediscovering old passions we left by the wayside or finding entirely new interests that ignite a spark within us. It can mean connecting with what makes us feel alive and purposeful, whether that's through creative expression, helping others, engaging in community service, or pursuing a long-held dream. Tapping into the activities and goals can make us feel genuinely alive and fulfilled. It's the feeling you get when you create something beautiful, make a positive impact on someone else's life, or reach a goal you've worked hard for. These pursuits give our lives depth and meaning, creating a sense of accomplishment, self-respect and pride that drink, and drugs could never provide.

Finding purpose in recovery often involves contributing positively to those around us and the wider community. It shifts our narrative from struggle to resilience and service. By focusing on what we can give rather than what we lack, we enrich our own lives and positively impact others. This sense of contribution reinforces our recovery, as it aligns with the values of compassion, gratitude, and connection. Finding purpose is a deeply personal journey and can vary from person to person. However, there are ten general steps and considerations to help us on this path.

1. Self-Reflection:

The heart of the matter - We start with a pause. We take a moment away from the hustle and bustle to really think about what lights us up inside. What activities make us lose track of time? We recall those moments when we felt truly alive and full of good energy. These aren't just happy memories; they're signposts pointing towards our purpose.

2. Identifying Our Passions And Interests:

Our inner compass - Now we think about what gets us excited. Is there a cause or an issue that really grabs us? Is there an activity or pastime that makes us feel like we could conquer the world? That's our heart speaking. The sweet spot for our life's purpose often lies in what we love doing and what we're good at. It's like finding a secret door where our heart's desires and our skills meet.

3. Consider Your Talents And Strengths:

The built in toolbox - Everyone of us has something we're naturally good at. Some of us may be a whiz with numbers, or others make people laugh until their sides hurt. These talents are our personal toolbox for making a difference in the world. Recognising and using these tools can lead us closer to our purpose.

4. Experiment and Explore:

The Adventure begins - Adventure time! Step out of your comfort zone and try new things. Ever thought about learning to paint, or a writer (this is my first time!!!!) a musician or a singer? Go for it! New experiences widen our horizons and might just uncover a passion we never knew existed.

5. Seek Feedback And Mentorship:

Navigating with Guidance - Chat with people you trust about your search for purpose. These conversations can act like mirrors reflecting our deepest desires and potential within us. Friends, family, and mentors can provide insights we might not have considered. Their encouragement and advice can be the nudge we need to move forward in our journey.

6. Look For The Intersections Of Your Passions And The World's Needs:

Where the magic happens - True purpose often lives at the crossroads of our deepest passions and the world's greatest needs becomes a calling. When our passions align with making a difference in the world, we're on to something really special. It becomes more than just a passion it becomes our personal calling card to making a positive impact on the world around us.

7. Set Goals And Take Action:

Small steps big leaps - Understanding our purpose is only the beginning. The real magic happens when we translate this knowledge into action. Setting small, achievable goals allows us to make progress step by step towards our larger vision. Each step forward clarifies our purpose, setting in stone our commitment to the journey ahead.

8. Be Patient And Open To Change:

The journey unfolds - Remember, finding our purpose isn't a one-off event, it's an evolving journey that unfolds over a lifetime. As we grow and change, so too may our purpose. We must be open to new paths and ideas as we grow and learn more about ourselves. Our purpose might shift and change, and that's okay—it's all part of the adventure. Embracing new experiences and insights, ensures that our lives remain aligned with our most authentic selves.

9. Practice Mindfulness And Gratitude:

Stay grounded - We must stay present and thankful for were we are right now. This is exactly where we are meant to be. Mindfulness and gratitude can keep us grounded and appreciative of the journey, even when the destination feels a bit foggy. By appreciating where we are, we open ourselves to the possibilities that lie ahead, ready to embrace whatever comes our way with grace and gratitude.

10. Contribute To Others:

The Ripple Effect - The most important expression of purpose is when we start to use our talents to help others. Our sense of purpose gets supercharged. By leveraging our strengths in service of others, we not only find deeper meaning in our own lives but also contribute to a ripple effect of positive change. It's in these moments of contribution that we find our purpose shining brightly. This legacy is perhaps the most enduring testament to a life well-lived.

Discovering our purpose is a deeply personal and evolving journey, unique to each of us. It's perfectly natural not to have all the answers immediately; finding our true calling unfolds over time through our experiences, the reflections we ponder, and our interactions with the wider world. In recovery, the search for purpose is about building a life that genuinely reflects who we are—a life rich with passion, imbued with meaning, and vibrant with connections. This path isn't always easy, but it's deeply rewarding, offering us a life we've intentionally shaped, brimming with endless possibilities. This newfound purpose does more than just occupy the space left by addiction; it propels us toward a future bright with the potential for growth, brimming with joy, and ripe with fulfillment. This pursuit is not just part of our recovery; it nourishes our soul and transforms our existence.

CHAPTER SEVEN SUMMARY

Embarking on the Recovery Journey:

Recovery starts with both apprehension and optimism. This phase marks a significant change, moving away from old habits and towards new possibilities, filled with both challenge and excitement.

Committing to Plan A:

In recovery, there's only one plan: Plan A. It represents an unwavering commitment to the recovery process, recognizing that moving forward is the only way through.

Navigating Recovery's Challenges:

The journey of recovery is comparable to navigating a ship through tumultuous seas. It's difficult and demanding but teaches resilience and the strength to overcome adversity.

Reflective Growth:

Recovery involves looking back to learn from past mistakes, making amends, and embracing self-forgiveness, which are fundamental for personal growth and moving forward.

Managing Emotional Challenges:

Handling intense emotions effectively is crucial. Adopting healthy coping mechanisms like exercise, journalling and open conversations helps manage emotional turbulence without being overwhelmed.

Overcoming Temptations and Old Habits:

Essential to recovery is the avoidance of old triggers and maintaining focus on sobriety. It involves strategic avoidance of previous influences and steadfast dedication to new habits.

Rebuilding Trust:

One of the most challenging aspects of recovery is rebuilding trust. It requires consistent effort and integrity to heal relationships and demonstrate personal change.

Daily Commitment to Sobriety:

Every day in recovery involves a conscious decision to stay sober. This includes managing cravings, maintaining healthy habits, and seeking opportunities for personal growth.

Finding Purpose Beyond Sobriety:

Recovery is not just about staying clean; it's about finding a deeper purpose that gives life meaning. This involves discovering new passions, continuous learning, and contributing positively to the community, thereby enriching one's life with fulfillment and a sense of achievement.

Main Points Chapter Seven:

Recovery demands a solid commitment to facing past actions, managing emotions, and resisting old temptations. It's a daily dedication to sobriety and personal growth, requiring us to rebuild trust and discover new purposes. This transformative journey enriches our lives, providing a deeper understanding of ourselves and filling us with renewed hope and fulfilment.

BEYOND RECOVERY -APPLYING SIMPLICITY IN LIFE

Our world is flooded with complexity, volatility, and constant noise. In contrast, the concept of simplicity offers a beacon of hope, promising peace and clarity. As we find ourselves lost in the relentless pace of daily commitments and digital deluge that fuel a frenzy within us, the yearning for a simpler, more meaningful life grows stronger. In simpler terms, the idea of simplicity is not just about how things look or following a trend. It has a deeper significance and impact. It becomes an essential framework for breaking down the chaos of modern life, guiding us toward genuine fulfilment. By embracing simplicity, we embark on a transformative journey to streamline our surroundings, thoughts, and relationships, shedding the excess to focus on what truly matters. This path encourages us to reevaluate our priorities and commitments, cultivating a life that reflects our deepest values and aspirations.

A cluttered life once muffled my inner voice, making it difficult to understand my emotions and those of others. My journey toward simplicity started as a way to manage recovery's complexities but evolved into a life blueprint. By simplifying daily life, I tuned into my emotions with greater clarity. Stripping away the unnecessary taught me to listen more attentively to both my feelings and those around me, laying the foundation for emotional intelligence. Emotional intelligence—the ability to understand, manage, and express my emotions and handle relationships effectively—flourished in this simplified environment. It fosters a deeper understanding of why I can feel what I feel and how my emotions influence my thoughts and actions. In simplicity, I found the space to reflect, to understand my emotional responses, and to choose to show up to the world around me.

Choosing simplicity doesn't mean giving up modern conveniences; it means being mindful and deliberate in our actions and choices. It calls us to clear out the clutter from both our spaces and our minds, which helps us focus better, be more creative, and find peace. In our relationships, it's about valuing deep, genuine connections that nourish our soul. By focusing on what's truly important, we free up our time and energy for things that really matter to us, leading to a happier and more meaningful life. Simplicity, therefore, offers a road map for intentional living, a map that leads us to a place where we can experience calm, happiness and real satisfaction.

THE QUIET REVOLUTION: EMBRACING SIMPLICITY

Imagine for a moment a life where we're not always running against time, but instead, each day is a fresh start, ready to be filled with things that really matter. This isn't just some daydream, it's something we can actually make happen by embracing simplicity. Simplicity isn't just about having fewer things or having less just for the sake of it, it's about making room for the stuff that brings real value and happiness into our lives. It means choosing the good stuff over just lots of stuff, focusing on what's truly important and vibrant. Choosing simplicity can make us happier, improve relationships, and increase life satisfaction. For starters, it can help clear our minds from all the clutter of wanting more and meeting everyone's expectations. This clarity gives us peace, lets us concentrate on our dreams, the people we love, and what we enjoy doing most. Having a simpler space to live in can also lower our stress and give us a calm place for everyday life. Plus, living simply can save us money since we're happy with what we have and not always wanting more. All these benefits together can lead us to a life that's more real and filled with joy, based on meaningful experiences and deep connections instead of just owning a lot of stuff.

Starting with simplicity involves evaluating what we own and how we spend our time, asking if these things truly add value to our lives. We need to think about cleaning out not just our closets but also our digital clutter and the things we feel obligated to do. We should be mindful about what we buy, thinking about its impact on our lives and the world. It also means learning to say no sometimes, setting limits to keep our energy and time focused on what's truly important. Adopting routines that simplify our daily tasks can open up room for more creativity and unplanned fun.

As we get rid of the extra and concentrate on the must haves, we start seeing amazing changes. Life gets more colourful, filled with real joy and new discoveries. Our relationships get stronger because we have the space and time to really care for them. Our creativity can soar without all the distractions, fuelled by the clear-headedness that comes with simplicity. Plus, we're doing the planet a favour by reducing what we use and waste. In the end, simplifying our life brings us a kind of freedom that's about breaking free from all the stuff and finding endless opportunities to grow, be happy, and truly fulfilled.

In short, simplicity isn't just a choice of how to live; it's a powerful journey that changes what we give importance to, boosts our well-being, and deeply enriches our lives. It challenges us to think about what's really key for us and to make room for those things, promising a way of life that's more meaningful, filled with joy, and utterly genuine.

SIMPLIFYING YOUR SPACE: OUR HOME IS OUR HAVEN.

We have touched on this previously in Chapters Two and Three, but I feel it's important to look at it again in the context of applying simplicity to our lives. Our homes are so much more than just buildings; they're where we find comfort and calm. Our homes can be havens. Simplifying our living spaces is an age-old concept that remains relevant for creating a peaceful, organized environment. This whole process starts right at home, turning cluttered rooms into peaceful spots that reflect an internal sense of calmness. We looked at the messy room earlier, with stuff all over the place. This mess can actually show what's going on inside us – a mix of stress, too much to do, and being pulled in too many directions. The clutter isn't just about having too many things; it's like a picture of the mess in our minds. By realising this, we see that making our space simpler helps clear up our thoughts, leading to a clearer head and more peace.

Getting rid of clutter is more than just cleaning up; it's a deep dive into figuring out what really matters to us. When we decide to let go of stuff, it's like we're saying we're done carrying around things we don't need. This isn't just about whether something is useful or makes us happy; it's a chance to think about what's truly important to us. By keeping only what matters or brings us joy, we're not just cleaning up our homes; we're making our lives simpler. Decluttering is a form of self-care, affirming that we deserve to live in a space that feels good. It's about turning our home into a personal oasis that helps us feel well. This change isn't just about organising things, it's about claiming our space as our own, a safe spot where we can relax, recharge, and be our best selves.

The good things that come from making our space simpler are huge. It's not just about having a neat house; it's about how that neatness makes the rest of our lives better. A tidy space helps us feel calm and organised, makes it easier to focus and get things done, and is a way to practice mindfulness, helping us enjoy the present and appreciate the simple things around us. In the end, making our living space simpler is a journey to find out what really matters to us. It encourages us to think about what's essential, to let go of what's not, and to value our living spaces. This journey isn't just for looks; it's about creating a lifestyle that brings peace, happiness, and well-being. By choosing to simplify, we bring balance into our lives and turn our homes into true sanctuaries where we can thrive.

SIMPLIFYING RELATIONSHIPS: THE ESSENCE OF GENUINE CONNECTIONS

In our fast paced digitally dominated world forming relationships and connections to other heart beats can be tricky and complicated. As we evolve as humans its seems that we are creating more complexity, more noise, more stress in modern relationships. Yet we are also seeing more and more people trying to make things simpler. This doesn't mean cutting down the number of friends we have but rather focusing on building stronger, more meaningful relationships. In today's digital world, where it's easy to confuse a Social Media interaction for a deep conversation, choosing to deepen our connections with a few people is kind of revolutionary. As we evolve, it seems we've become more and more entangled in an ever-complex web of interactions, bombarded by a constant stream of notifications and digital chatter. This noise, this relentless buzz, adds layers of complexity and stress to our relationships, making it increasingly difficult to find and nurture genuine connections amidst the racket. Simplifying our relationships means choosing to spend our time and energy on people who really get us, support us, and help us grow, creating bonds that really last.

Yet, in the middle of all this chaos, there's a growing movement towards simplification. This isn't about reducing the number of people in our lives but about enriching the quality of our connections. In a world where a quick text often substitutes for a heartfelt dialogue, making the conscious decision to foster deeper relationships is both radical and necessary. Simplifying our relational world means investing our time and energy into people who truly understand us, offer support, and encourage our growth. It's about creating bonds that aren't just short lived but are built to last. We live in a hyper-connected world. The rise of social media and instant messaging has changed how we connect with each other. Sure, it's easier than ever to stay connected, but this constant connection can sometimes make us feel more alone, not less. More isolated and less connected at a human level. With so many superficial interactions, it's tough to find those deeper, more meaningful connections where we feel truly understood. This challenge is about figuring out how to have meaningful relationships in a world that's always online.

The real magic happens when we decide to focus on those deeper connections. Simplifying our relationships doesn't mean we're isolating ourselves or withdrawing into solitude. Instead, it's about being picky in a good way, surrounding ourselves with people who really matter to us. It's about intentionally selecting and surrounding ourselves with people who share our joys, understand our struggles and stand by us through thick and thin. This choice to focus on quality over quantity lets us have more meaningful conversations, shared experiences, and genuine support, laying the foundation for friendships that really last. To build meaningful connections, identify the important people in your life and make an effort to be actively involved. It's about setting clear boundaries, having honest conversations, doing fun and meaningful activities together, and really listening to each other. These steps help us move past the small talk and build relationships that are all about understanding, supporting, and genuinely caring for each other. This can be challenging, uncomfortable at times, it can make us feel uneasy and vulnerable, yet all of these sensations are the building blocks of deep sustainable and enriching relationships. Nothing good comes easy, we have to work for it.

The payoff for simplifying our relationships is massive. These deep connections give us a sense of belonging, cuts down on loneliness, and contributes positively to our overall happiness and wellbeing. This is what living is really about, bonding with others we care for and who care for us. They're the people we turn to for inspiration, support, and comfort, showing just how important genuine friendships are in our lives. Nothing superficial, no sham connections just simply real.

To sum it all up, choosing to focus on deep, meaningful relationships in the hustle and bustle of modern life is much more than just personal preference, it's a statement. It's a commitment to choosing depth, meaning, and realness over just having lots of friends or followers. We choose authenticity over pretentious and hollow associations. By putting effort into these genuine connections, we make our own lives better and help create a world that's more connected and caring. So, let's make it a point to build and cherish these deep bonds. They're what make life rich, happy, and truly fulfilling. By getting a handle on what makes these connections work and how to foster them, we're all set to steer our relationships in a way that brings more joy and meaning into our lives and the lives of those we care about.

SIMPLIFYING WELLNESS: A HOLISTIC APPROACH

The journey towards simplicity also encompasses our physical and mental health. In an age of trends and quick fixes, simplicity returns us to fundamentals: nourishing food, regular movement, restful sleep, and mindfulness. This holistic approach emphasizes the importance of listening to our bodies and nurturing them with kindness and respect. Simplifying wellness means making conscious choices that support our overall well-being, allowing us to live fully and vibrantly. We see on social media, TV etc, where quick health fixes and the latest fads take centre stage, but these so called next best things can end up causing more harm than good to our bodies and minds. Finding the true meaning of wellness can feel very complicated. Amidst this bombardment of advice and trends, the idea of keeping things simple stands out. It guides us back to the basics that truly nurture both our bodies and minds.

Simplifying wellness isn't about jumping on the latest diet bandwagon or pushing ourselves through intense workout routines that don't last. It's about adopting a holistic approach that respects the natural intelligence of our bodies and the rhythms of life. This way of thinking pushes us to make choices that genuinely support our well-being, allowing us to live lives filled with energy and clear purpose.

One of the basics of simplifying wellness is nourishment. It's about feeding our bodies the kind of food they're designed to thrive on, steering clear of the complex and often contradictory dietary trends. Being healthy means feeling good about who you are. Ignore those unrealistic body images you see on social media or magazines. There is an eating plan that always gets results. It's called a balanced eating plan, simple. It's nothing new it's been around forever. Simplifying our diet means going back to the basics, enjoying whole, unprocessed foods like fruits, vegetables, whole grains, lean proteins, and healthy fats. The sort of food I would have eaten daily when I was growing up in Ireland in the 60's and 70's.

This approach doesn't box us into strict eating rules but allows us to listen to our bodies, choosing foods that make us feel alive and energetic rather than restricted. Nourishment is more than just food, what we consume effects all of our internal systems. The food we eat is more than just fuel. It's the basis of a transportation system that carries nutrients, energy, information, throughout our body. It is a connection system that links the various systems in our body. Our gut is the home of billions of bacteria. The food we eat directly impacts these bacteria which in turn influences the production of neurotransmitters. Ninety percent of serotonin receptors which regulate our mood that in turn influences our biological and neurological processes such as aggression, anxiety, cognition, mood, and sleep — are located in the gut. Food can trigger changes in our physiology associated with emotions, food can influence our heart rate, body temperature. Certain foods can make us feel well whilst others make us sick. Simply put a balanced diet keeps this incredibly complex system balanced!

Human beings are designed to move, yet we have become a sedentary society spending most of our time sitting. Simplifying wellness reshapes our view of physical activity, it's about seeing exercise not as a chore we have to squeeze into our busy schedules or as a punishment for eating certain foods, but as a natural part of our daily life that actually brings joy and happiness. Think of movement as an opportunity to feel good, whether it's a dance class that makes us lose track of time, a yoga session that leaves us feeling grounded and centred, or a simple walk in nature that clears our mind, exercise should be something we look forward to, a way to connect with our bodies and appreciate our strength and agility.

Exercise boosts endorphins and dopamine, which enhance happiness, confidence, and capability, while reducing anxiety and stress. It's about finding types of movement that we genuinely enjoy, When we focus on the happiness movement brings, rather than obsessing over calories burned, number of steps or miles run, staying active becomes a joyful part of life rather than a punishment. Movement as a natural, enjoyable part of our daily routine is about more than just exercise. It's about creating a life where happiness, health, and a sense of well-being become part of our everyday existence. It's about moving because it makes us feel alive, connected, and vibrant, because it's simply what we were made to do.

Sleep is another crucial piece of the wellness puzzle. Embracing simplicity means making sleep a priority, understanding that it's as important as what we eat and how we move. This might involve creating a peaceful bedtime routine, making our sleep space as comfy as possible, and sticking to a consistent sleeping schedule. By giving our body the rest it needs, we're supporting everything from our immune system to our mental sharpness and emotional stability.

Mindfulness is at the heart of mental wellness. In a world that often prizes doing multiple things at once and constantly being on the go, mindfulness teaches us the power of slowing down and being fully present. This could be through meditation, focusing on our breath, or simply immersing ourselves fully in whatever we're doing. Mindfulness helps us watch our thoughts and feelings from a distance, promoting a sense of inner calm and connection that's essential for our mental and emotional well-being.

Simplifying wellness is about more than just avoiding sickness; it's about fostering a life that's vibrant, meaningful, and joyful. It encourages us to tune into our bodies, to live mindfully, and to make choices that truly feed our overall health. By doing so, we find that wellness isn't a fixed goal but a path, one marked by simplicity, equilibrium, and a deep connection to the joy of living. This approach turns simplicity from just a concept into a daily practice, helping us face life's complexities with grace and energy. In embracing this journey towards simplified wellness, we're not just cutting out the noise; we're amplifying what truly matters. It's a commitment to living in a way that's both grounded and inspired, making every day an opportunity to nourish, move, rest, and connect in ways that bring us genuine fulfilment.

Simplifying wellness is about rediscovering the power of listening to our bodies, of moving for pleasure, of sleeping deeply, and of being fully present in each moment. It's a path to not just a healthier life, but a richer, more vibrant existence.

SIMPLIFYING TECHNOLOGY: THE ART OF DISCONNECTION

We are inundated with a never ending stream of digital rattle and distraction. What was initially meant to serve us, to improve our quality of life has become the thief of our attention. Everywhere we go it's all around us. Hordes of people like drones walking along with their faces constantly in a screen. And it has happened so fast. There are those of us young enough who cannot remember what is was like before. Who cannot comprehend how we could have lived our lives without this ubiquitous technology. And yet we did. That was before the constant din of never ending digital information, apps, notifications and buzzing devices constantly demanding and consuming our attention. Addictive algorithms fuel a frenzy of outrage, anxiety, fear, hate and belligerence. All of this creates unrealistic expectation that we put upon ourselves and others -the ideal life, the ideal relationship, the ideal home and ideal family which all exist in the ideal virtual world. It has our minds where it wants them, it's a thief of our attention and the more we consume the stronger the grip it has on us, a never ending steam of stimulus and excitement (both good and bad). All of this at the expense of our peace of mind.

It's overwhelming, cluttering our lives with unnecessary digital noise disguised as must have information. Prodding us to get the next feel good sensation from all the likes we got on our most recent post. We crave this digital validation but at what cost. It's no wonder we have a global mental health problem. The algorithms and the companies behind them do not want you to have peace of mind. They don't want you to experience the simple beauty of quiet. If your quiet, they haven't got you. When you're experiencing simplicity, they haven't got you. When you are connected to another heartbeat in a deep and meaningful way they haven't got you.

Often, our gadgets go from being helpful tools to extensions of our own bodies. We don't just use technology; we live by it. What was supposed to be an innovation designed to serve us has turned us into servants of it. This constant use can lead to several problems, like stress, sleep issues, and a shortened attention span. Simplifying our digital life means setting boundaries with our technology use, making sure that we control our devices instead of letting them control us. But you are free to choose. Be a slave to the Digital Master or be The Master of your true self.

So how do we go about reducing all of this techno clutter in our lives. Learning and practising digital disconnection, simplifying our technology use is not only critical for our mental clarity it's also crucial for our emotional wellbeing. What are some simple actions we can take to simplify our technology usage. I have set out five simple and straight forward steps to reclaim our attention and become the master of our usage and not a slave to it.

1. Digital Detox:

Set aside specific times each day—like during meals, the first hour after you wake up, or right before bed—when you'll stay off digital devices. This break from technology helps you enjoy the moment and connect more with the world around you.

2. Prioritise Face-to-Face Interaction:

Choose in-person conversations over texts or emails. Real-life interactions are often more meaningful than online ones and can help you build stronger, more genuine relationships.

3. Create Tech-Free Zones:

Designate areas in your home, like the bedroom or dining room, where digital devices are not allowed. This helps turn these spaces into peaceful sanctuaries for relaxation and mindfulness.

4. Conscious Consumption:

Manage your digital intake as carefully as you would your diet. Unsubscribe from unnecessary newsletters, delete apps you don't use, and customise your social media feeds to only show content that truly benefits you.

5. Intentional Technology Use

Use your devices purposefully rather than passively. Instead of mindlessly scrolling, use technology for specific tasks like learning new skills, staying connected with family, or organising your work.

Taking breaks from technology can greatly improve our life. It helps us focus better and increase our productivity by giving us undisturbed time to think and work. Emotionally, it can reduce the anxiety that comes from constant connectivity. Physically, we sleep better and suffer less eye strain. And socially, it can improve our relationships by encouraging more meaningful interactions. The aim of simplifying our technology use isn't to give up our devices entirely but to find a balance. Technology should support our life, not run it. By setting limits on our technology use, we can make room for personal growth, build stronger relationships, and reconnect with the natural world—a refreshing change from the digital landscape.

So in essence simplifying our digital life by learning to disconnect isn't about rejecting modern tools but about enhancing our quality of life. It's about being in charge of our digital interactions so that we can enjoy richer, more fulfilling experiences in every part of our life. By setting these boundaries, we ensure that we live as the director of our technology, not its lackey.

SIMPLIFYING LEISURE: REDISCOVERING SIMPLE JOYS

We have come to associate leisure with expensive, exclusive and extravagant activities and experiences. We are inundated with ads for luxury resorts, exclusive spa breaks or even luxury cruises around exotic islands. Now don't get me wrong I am in no way adverse to any of these, yet while these activities are wonderful and offer unique experiences there is a cost. And this cost can make us feel more burdened, both in our wallets and in our minds. Yet we tend to overlook leisure and relaxation that comes from simpler, more traditional activities. By focusing more on these leisure and relaxation approaches we can make our downtime more fulfilling.

In Chapter Three we delved into the benefits of minimalism in recovery. We looked at the concept of decluttering. We can apply this concept of decluttering to how we choose to spend our free time. By purposefully choosing simpler and cheaper activities (in some cases they are free!), we can effectively decrease our stress levels and increase our quality relaxation time. This minimalist approach means we choose quality over quantity, opting for activities that are less resource intensive (i.e. hit our wallets) but more personally rewarding. Let's look at some of these simple activities that return a much great dividend for our investment in them.

Nature Walks:

A simple walk outside, whether it's in a bustling city park or on a quiet mountain trail, provides both physical exercise and a mental refresh. Breathing in the fresh air listening to the sounds of nature around us as we walk along a trail is one of the richest leisure activities we can experience. During the different seasons of the year this simple walk through the same trail delivers a multitude of sensory stimuli. In winter we can experience the crispy air and the quite of the bare trees. In autumn we are witness to a blaze of foliage colours and animal activity as they prepare their store for the coming winter. In spring we witness the scene coming back to life we smell the budding plants and wildflowers, the movement of the animals that have come back after their winter sleep. And in summer we feel the heat of the sun on the lush grass under our feet while the pollen bees busy buzzing from flower to flower collecting the nectar to bring home to the hive, Connecting with nature lowers your stress levels and improves your focus and presence. Simple and wonderful this type of leisure activity is food for our soul.

Reading:

In our digital-heavy world, sitting down with a good book is a rare treat. Reading is a simple way to relax and learn something new, providing a peaceful break from the noise of everyday life. There is something wonderful, tangible and comforting in holding a printed book. The feel of turning each of the printed pages and the smell of the paper, sometimes fresh if newly printed, sometimes stirring up memories of times gone by if an older novel. It engages all of our senses. When you read, you dive into different worlds and meet new characters, fuelling your imagination in ways that movies or television simply can't match. You get to imagine the landscapes, hear the voices, and feel the emotions of the tales you read, all at your own pace and in your own way. This stokes the fires of your creativity, providing a mental workout that is both stimulating and relaxing.

Reading is a quiet and enriching activity, taking time out to be with a book is one of the great leisure pastimes of life. Whether you buy books or borrow them from a library. The cost is minimal compared to many other activities and form of entertainment. Taking time out to read isn't just another way to pass the time, it's one of life's genuine pleasures. Reading a book is a solitary activity that allows you to slow down, reflect, and grow internally. It's a decision. So, in our fast-paced, app-driven lives, making the choice to pick up a book and read can be a radical act of self-care and simplicity. It's a decision to disconnect from the noise around us and engage with a story or a set of ideas on a deep, personal level. Reading enriches our lives, broadens our horizons, and strengthens the mental capacity we need to face the complexity of the modern world.

Creative Pursuits:

Activities like drawing, writing, or making music is more than just a way to fill time. It not only keep our minds sharp but also give us a deep sense of personal achievement. I can testify to this personally as writing this book has been a truly transformative process for me. I have used the writing as a sanctuary from the daily grind at times. It has gifted me a space where my mind roamed free, explored all of the ideas and concepts on my recovery. Writing helped me reflect even deeper on my own experience in recovery without constraint. It became a gateway to a deeper understanding of myself and the world around me. It has provided me with the privilege to share my experience with you the reader. For this I am very grateful.

Creative activities require a level of focus that can act as a form of meditation. When we're immersed in creating something, our mind tends to shed the stress and clutter of everyday life. After a while we notice that we find ourselves in that flow state. Just there with the activity. This concentration can clear our thoughts, allowing us to become absorbed in the details of our creative work. The repetitive actions of sketching lines, choosing words, or adjusting chords can serve as a mindfulness practice that calms the mind.

Participating in creative activities like art, writing, or music delivers us numerous benefits beyond simple enjoyment. These activities provide a vital outlet for expressing and processing complex emotions, making it easier to handle tough experiences and gain personal insights. Creating something unique, from a piece of art, music or writing, boosts self-esteem and builds confidence as each completed project feels like a personal victory. These activities can create within us a lifelong habit of learning and curiosity, as they encourage us to continuously explore new ideas and master new skills. Participating in creative communities can deepen social connections, helping us build relationships with like-minded individuals which can enrich our social life and provide emotional support. Creative works can serve as a lasting legacy, capturing our thoughts and emotions and impacting others long after they are created. These benefits make creative pursuits a powerful tool for personal development and fulfilment.

To sum this up, simplifying our leisure time encourages us to rediscover the joy in simple pleasures. In a culture that often equates leisure with consumption and extravagance, simplicity invites us to find satisfaction in nature walks, reading, and creative pursuits. These activities, grounded in the present moment, offer us relief from the hustle and bustle, nurturing our souls and sparking genuine happiness.

THE PATH AHEAD: LIVING SIMPLY IN A COMPLEX WORLD

As we continue down the path of simplicity, we come to understand that decluttering our lives and prioritizing what truly matters are not mere one-time events, but rather dynamic, ongoing processes. This journey into simplicity demands constant vigilance and introspection, inviting us to continually reassess our possessions, our activities, and even our relationships. The goal is to strip away the unnecessary, leaving room only for what truly adds value to our lives. This ongoing cycle of reflection and realignment helps us to focus on our core desires and to eliminate distractions that cloud our purpose.

In embracing a simpler life, we commit to a lifestyle of thoughtful choices. Each decision we make—from the things we buy to the commitments we accept—is guided by a deeper understanding of what we truly value. This isn't about denying oneself enjoyment or luxury; rather, it's about finding joy and luxury in the simplicity of well-chosen and meaningful pursuits. Living intentionally in this way allows us to align our daily actions with our long-term goals, making every moment count towards a fuller, more satisfying life.

The quiet revolution of simplicity offers us something profoundly counter-cultural in today's fast-paced, consumer-driven world. It does not guarantee an easy life free from troubles. Instead, it prepares us to face life's inevitable challenges with a clearer mind and a stronger spirit. The clarity that comes from a simplified life enables us to see challenges not as obstacles but as opportunities to grow and learn. Meanwhile, the resilience we build by focusing on what truly matters provides the strength to push through difficulties with grace.

By choosing simplicity, we choose a richer life—one marked by deep, fulfilling experiences and genuine connections. This richness comes not from an accumulation of goods, but from a wealth of experiences—quiet moments of joy, deep conversations, and shared adventures that resonate with our soul. Simplicity, therefore, doesn't just simplify our external circumstances; it enriches our inner lives, offering peace and contentment that endure beyond the transient satisfaction of material possessions. This is the true essence of living a life of simplicity—finding abundance in the quality of our experiences rather than the quantity of our possessions.

CHAPTER EIGHT SUMMARY

Embracing Simplicity as a Lifestyle:

The chapter calls for simplicity as a way to manage the complexity and chaos of modern life. It highlights how adopting a simpler lifestyle helps focus on what's truly important—our values and aspirations.

Emotional Intelligence and Simplification:

Simplifying life is shown to enhance emotional intelligence by allowing for clearer emotional understanding and expression, facilitating better interpersonal relationships.

Mindful Living:

Highlights the importance of mindfulness in daily choices, advocating for decluttering both physical and mental spaces to improve focus, creativity, and peace.

Value of Deep Connections:

The text encourages nurturing deep, meaningful relationships rather than superficial digital interactions, emphasising the importance of quality over quantity in social bonds.

Benefits of a Simple Life:

Key benefits discussed include reduced stress, increased happiness, and more meaningful personal connections, all contributing to a more fulfilling life.

Holistic Wellness:

Simplicity extends to wellness by advocating for natural, fundamental practices like nutritious eating, regular physical activity, adequate sleep, and mindfulness to enhance overall well-being.

Reducing Digital Overload:

The chapter advises on managing technology use to prevent it from overwhelming our lives, suggesting practical steps like digital detoxes and creating tech-free zones.

Simplifying Leisure:

Spotlights returning to simple, traditional leisure activities like nature walks, reading, and creative pursuits that provide joy without the burdens of high cost or extravagance.

Main Points Chapter Eight:

This chapter sets out the great benefits of applying the principles of simplicity beyond recovery into all areas of our lives. It presents simplicity not just as a way to organise physical space but as a holistic approach that enhances emotional intelligence, deepens personal relationships, and promotes overall well-being. The chapter calls for intentional living through mindful choices that prioritise genuine connections and meaningful experiences over material abundance. By focusing on simplicity, we can find greater clarity, peace, and fulfilment in a complex, uncertain and volatile world, transforming our daily lives into a more purposeful and joyous living experience.

CHAPTER 9

SUMMING IT UP

We have journeyed together through the transformative power of simplicity, a beacon that guides us back to the essentials of life. This book is not just a guide, it's an invitation to rediscover the profound joy and clarity that come from stripping away the nonessential noise and complexity that plagues our lives in addiction. It speaks directly to those of us who are in recovery and or about to embark on the road to recovery. It is also intended to resonate with anyone seeking a more meaningful existence. The core message is clear, simplicity is not merely about reducing the clutter in our physical spaces but about reshaping our entire approach to life. It's about finding beauty in less, finding strength in quietness, and making intentional choices that align with our deepest values and aspirations.

Recovery is a journey that often feels overwhelming. The prospect of changing lifelong habits and facing a future without dependency can seem daunting, if not outright impossible. In the heart of the book there is a stirring focus on the practice of taking recovery one day at a time. This is where the wisdom of simplifying the process to "one day at a time" becomes invaluable. It breaks down the vast challenge of recovery into achievable, daily actions. Each day is a new opportunity to maintain sobriety, to make choices that support physical and emotional health, and to engage in activities that enrich one's spirit. This principle is foundational in the journey of recovery, emphasizing that the path to healing and simplicity isn't about making huge leaps overnight but about steady, small, manageable steps every day. I have set out the fundamental principles and transformative insights from "Keep It Simple" below.

MINDFULNESS AND PRESENCE

The book teaches that mindfulness is key in the one-day-at-a-time approach. Being fully present each day allows us to focus on our current feelings and needs without the added pressure of past regrets or future anxieties. This daily practice of mindfulness fosters a deeper understanding of our emotions and triggers, empowering us to manage them proactively. It helps us resist the trap of emotional time travelling keeping us rooted in the now. Below is a practical exercise you can try. Integrating mindfulness into your recovery can be both simple and profound. One effective method is the **Five-Minute Breathing Space Exercise**, which you can practice anywhere at any time to center yourself and connect with the present.

- **Find a Quiet Spot:** Choose a quiet location where you won't be disturbed. Sit comfortably, keeping your back straight and feet on the ground.

- **Observe Your Breath:** Close your eyes and focus on your breathing. Notice the air moving in and out of your body, the rise and fall of your chest, without trying to alter your breath.

- **Recognize Thoughts and Feelings:** As you concentrate on breathing, thoughts and emotions will surface. Simply acknowledge these, without judgment, and gently redirect your attention back to your breath.

- **Widen Your Awareness:** After a few minutes, expand your awareness from your breathing to include bodily sensations and the environment around you—notice sounds, smells, and how your body feels in the space.

- **Conclude Gently:** To end, slowly move your fingers and toes, open your eyes, and take a moment to notice any changes in how you feel.

This brief exercise is a powerful tool for staying anchored in the present, helping to break the cycle of past regrets and future anxieties, and fostering a stronger, more focused recovery process.

DAILY REFLECTIONS AND INTENTIONS

Setting daily intentions is a powerful practice. By starting each day with a clear sense of purpose and a set of manageable goals, we can steer our day in a direction that supports our recovery and personal growth. Reflection at the end of the day allows us to acknowledge accomplishments, learn from challenges, and reset for the next day. I have set out below a practical example you can use daily. Here's a straightforward approach to integrating this practice into your daily routine.

Morning Intentions

- **Set Aside Time:** Dedicate five minutes each morning to this practice. Find a quiet place where you can sit undisturbed.

- **Write It Down:** On a notepad or in a journal, jot down one or two specific intentions for the day. These should be achievable and supportive of your recovery. For example, "Today, I will attend a support group meeting and spend at least 30 minutes reading a book."

- **Visualize Success:** Spend a moment visualizing yourself successfully fulfilling these intentions. Imagine how good you'll feel having achieved these goals.

Evening Reflection

- **Reflect on the Day:** In the evening, return to your notepad or journal. Reflect on how the day went regarding your morning intentions.

- **Acknowledge and Learn:** Write down any accomplishments and also note any challenges you encountered. Reflect on what you learned from both. For example, "Attending the support group provided me with great insights and connecting with others helped ease my anxiety."

- **Reset for Tomorrow:** Think about what you can carry forward to the next day. If there were setbacks, consider what adjustments might help.

This daily practice not only reinforces your commitment to recovery but also builds a structured approach to personal development. By setting clear intentions and reflecting on your daily experiences, you create a loop of continuous learning and achievement, helping to keep your recovery on a positive trajectory.

ROUTINE AND STRUCTURE

The simplicity of routine is celebrated as a cornerstone of daily recovery. Structured days with steady and predictable activities reduce stress and remove many uncertainties that can lead to anxiety and relapse. By establishing and sticking to a daily routine, we create a safe and supportive environment beneficial to recovery. Here's an example of how you can structure a day to foster a supportive environment for your recovery. Please note that all of our circumstances are different some of the examples below may not be applicable for all for various reasons and lifestyle constraints. It is important for all of us to seek structure and maintain routine in our daily lives.

Morning Routine

- **Wake Up at a Consistent Time:** Choose a time that allows you to start your day without rushing, setting a calm tone.

- **Morning Meditation or Prayer:** Spend 10-15 minutes in meditation or prayer to center yourself and set your intentions for the day.

- **Healthy Breakfast:** Nourish your body with a balanced breakfast to give you energy and improve concentration.

Midday Activities

- **Scheduled Therapy or Support Group:** Attend a therapy session or a support group meeting to connect with others and reinforce your commitment to recovery.

- **Physical Activity:** Engage in at least 30 minutes of physical activity, such as walking, yoga, or a workout at the gym. Exercise releases endorphins and improves overall well-being.

- **Lunch:** Have a healthy lunch to maintain energy levels throughout the day.

Afternoon Schedule

- **Focused Work or Volunteering:** Dedicate time to work or volunteer activities. This not only structures your afternoon but also provides a sense of purpose and achievement.

- **Mindful Breaks:** Take short breaks to practice mindfulness or relaxation techniques to stay centered and avoid burnout.

Evening Wind Down

- **Reflective Journaling:** Spend time writing in a journal to reflect on the day's successes and challenges. This can help process emotions and solidify lessons learned.

- **Healthy Dinner:** Prepare and enjoy a nutritious dinner, which plays a critical role in physical and mental health.

- **Relaxation Time:** Engage in a relaxing activity you enjoy, like reading, crafting, or listening to music, to wind down before bed.

Nighttime Routine

- **Prepare for the Next Day:** Lay out clothes for the next day, prepare any necessary items, and plan your breakfast and lunch.

- **Evening Meditation:** Before bed, practice another short meditation or prayer session to calm your mind and prepare for restful sleep.

- **Consistent Bedtime:** Go to bed at the same time each night to regulate your body's clock and ensure adequate rest.

EMOTIONAL AND PRACTICAL SUPPORT

The book stresses the importance of seeking support on a daily basis. Whether it's attending support group meetings, consulting with a therapist, or simply sharing with a trusted friend, regular engagement with supportive individuals provides strength and perspective. Real and meaningful physical connection is a powerful tool in the recovery tool kit. Here are some specific resources and types of support groups that can be particularly beneficial.

- **Alcoholics Anonymous (AA):** One of the most well-known support groups, AA offers a 12-step program designed to help individuals with alcohol addiction. Meetings are available in most communities around the world.

- **Narcotics Anonymous (NA):** Similar to AA, NA provides support for individuals recovering from drug addiction through a community-driven, 12-step program.

- **SMART Recovery:** This is a global community of mutual-support groups that offer a science-based program to help people recover from addictive behaviors. Unlike AA and NA, SMART Recovery focuses on self-empowerment and self-reliance.

- **Al-Anon/Alateen:** These groups provide support for family members and friends of individuals who have problems with alcohol. They focus on sharing experiences and learning effective ways to cope with the challenges of addiction.

- **Therapy and Counseling:** Engaging with a professional therapist or counselor who specializes in addiction recovery can provide personalized support and strategies tailored to individual needs.

- **Online Support Groups:** For those who may not have access to in-person meetings or prefer the anonymity of online spaces, there are numerous online support groups and forums that can provide encouragement and guidance.

- **Sober Living Communities:** These are residential facilities that provide a supportive, structured environment for people in recovery. Living in such a community can significantly help maintain sobriety, especially in the early stages of recovery.

- **Local Community Health Centers:** Many communities have health centers offering support groups, therapy, and workshops for individuals in recovery and their families.

- **Faith-based Groups:** Some people find strength and support in faith-based recovery programs offered by churches, mosques, synagogues, and other religious communities.

- **Recovery Coaching:** Recovery coaches provide one-on-one support and guidance through the recovery process, helping individuals navigate the challenges and milestones of sobriety.

Utilizing these resources can offer tremendous support and guidance, helping individuals in recovery build a network of care and accountability that can greatly enhance their journey toward a healthier, substance-free life.

GRATITUDE AND SMALL JOYS

One of the most transformative practices in the journey of recovery and personal growth is cultivating gratitude daily. Recognizing and appreciating the small victories and joys each day not only enriches our lives but also shifts our focus from what's missing to what's abundant and positive. Here are six steps for Gratitude Journalling to help you nurture gratitude every day.

1. **Choose a Time:** Set aside a few minutes each morning or evening for this practice. Consistency is key, so pick a time that easily fits into your daily routine.

2. **Create a Comfortable Space:** Find a quiet spot where you can sit comfortably without distractions. Having a dedicated space can enhance your focus and make the practice more meaningful.

3. **Keep a Journal:** Use a notebook or digital app specifically for this purpose. This will be your gratitude journal.

4. **Write Down Three Things:** Each day, write down three things for which you are grateful. These can be as simple as a warm cup of

coffee, a call from a friend, or a beautiful sunset you witnessed. The key is to find things that truly made you feel thankful that day.

5. **Elaborate on One:** Choose one of those three items and write a few more sentences about why you are grateful for it. This helps deepen your appreciation and reinforces the positive feelings associated with it.

6. **Reflect Periodically:** At the end of each week, take some time to review what you've written. Reflecting on your past entries can provide a powerful boost of positivity and a reminder of the good in your life, especially on tougher days.

This simple practice of gratitude journaling doesn't just help you recognize the good in your life; it actively shifts your mental focus from deficits to abundance, enhancing resilience and overall life satisfaction. Over time, as you make this practice a regular part of your day, you'll likely notice a more optimistic outlook and a greater sense of contentment in your life.

EMBRACE MINIMALISM

At its heart, minimalism goes beyond the façade of physical decluttering. It's about reducing the mental and emotional clutter that distracts us from our true paths. For those of us in recovery, this means creating an environment—both internally and externally—that supports sobriety and personal growth.

Before embracing minimalism, my life felt overwhelmingly cluttered, not just with physical items but with chaotic thoughts and unchecked emotions. In early recovery my environment was a reflection of my inner state—disorganized and filled with distractions that kept me from facing the deeper issues linked to my recovery. The turning point came in the middle of 2020 at the height of the Covid Pandemic lockdown. Like many I had transitioned to a remote working from home model. During a particularly stressful day I found myself unable to find a crucial document due to the state of my home office. This moment of frustration was a stark wake-up call about how my external clutter mirrored my internal turmoil. I decided it was time for a change, not just in my surroundings but in my approach to life.

I began by decluttering my home office space. Each item I chose to keep had to serve a purpose or bring me joy; everything else had to go. This process was surprisingly emotional—it wasn't just about discarding objects but about letting go of the fears and behaviors that had contributed to my addictive habits. As my physical space cleared, I noticed a shift in my mental state. I felt lighter and less anxious. The simplicity of my surroundings helped me focus on my recovery, making it easier to attend to my daily routines and self-care practices without the burden of excess. Embracing minimalism helped me understand that recovery is not just about abstaining from substances but about creating a life filled with meaning and intention. Reducing both my physical and mental clutter allowed me to focus on what truly matters—my health, my relationships, and my personal growth. Now, I find immense joy in the simplicity and clarity that minimalism brings, reaffirming my commitment to a sober, fulfilling life each day.

INTENTIONAL LIVING

Each chapter reinforces the idea that deliberate choices lead to a more authentic life. This is especially crucial in recovery, where every choice can be a step towards relapse or recovery. Living intentionally means actively shaping our lives and our environments in ways that foster health, happiness, and fulfilment. To help you make deliberate choices that lead to a more authentic life, here are specific actions and examples of intentional living that can make this concept more tangible and actionable for you:

- **Food and Drink:** Choose foods that nourish your body and mind. For instance, opt for water or herbal teas over sugary drinks and incorporate whole foods into your diet instead of processed items.

- **Morning Routine:** Start your day with a routine that sets a positive tone. This could include meditation, journaling, or a gentle workout. This practice helps establish a mindset focused on recovery and personal growth.

- **Evening Routine:** End your day on a reflective note, perhaps with gratitude journaling or a calming mindfulness exercise to ensure restful sleep and mental clarity.

- **Foster Supportive Connections:** Actively seek out and nurture relationships with people who support your recovery and encourage your growth. This might mean joining a recovery group or participating in community activities that align with your values.

- **Set Boundaries:** Learn to say no to situations and relationships that do not serve your best interests or that jeopardize your sobriety. If by chance someone reacts with hostility to your boundaries, then you know that they have found the edge where their respect for your boundaries ends.

- **Regular Meetings:** Whether it's a support group or therapy session, make a commitment to attend regularly. These meetings are vital checkpoints that keep you aligned with your recovery goals.

- **Learn a New Skill:** Engaging in learning not only occupies your mind and time constructively but also boosts your confidence as you see your abilities expand.

- **Read and Reflect:** Dedicate time to reading books that inspire and challenge you. Reflect on how the insights apply to your life and recovery.

These actions are not just tasks to check off; they are stepping stones to a richer, more fulfilling life. By living intentionally, you make choices every day that build a foundation for lasting recovery and true happiness. Begin with one or two of these suggestions, and as you integrate them into your life, you'll likely discover more ways to live authentically and purposefully.

VALUE QUALITY OVER QUANTITY

Whether it's the relationships we nurture, the possessions we own, or the activities we engage in, prioritising quality over quantity enriches our lives immeasurably. It teaches us to invest in meaningful interactions and choose pursuits that genuinely add value to our lives. Let's look at how Thomas benefited by adopting a quality over quantity approach to life. Thomas's journey is a compelling testament to the principle of valuing quality over quantity. For years, Thomas found himself caught in the whirlwind of a fast-paced lifestyle, accumulating friends, possessions, and experiences without pause. He measured his life's worth by its sheer volume: the number of social gatherings he attended, the array of gadgets he owned, and the endless stream of activities filling his calendar. Thomas lived his life from the outside in. Yet, despite the abundance, a profound sense of fulfillment eluded him. The turning point came during his recovery from addiction, a period when Thomas was forced to take stock of his life. He began by addressing his relationships. Previously, he had prided himself on his extensive circle of acquaintances, yet few were there for him during his most challenging times. He made a conscious decision to focus on nurturing deeper connections with a handful of people who truly cared about his well-being. These relationships, fewer in number but richer in depth, provided him with genuine support and a sense of community that had previously been missing.

Next, Thomas turned to his possessions. He cleared out his home, donating or discarding items that he had accumulated over the years, but which no longer served any purpose or brought him joy. This decluttering extended beyond the physical to the digital, where he reduced his engagement with social media, recognizing that it often left him feeling drained rather than enriched. In his activities, Thomas shifted his focus from being busy to being purposeful. He shifted to living his life from the inside out. He reduced his commitments, choosing to invest his time in activities that genuinely interested him or aided his recovery and personal growth. This included returning to his long-neglected hobby of painting and volunteering at a local community center, where he felt a meaningful impact on others and himself.

Through these changes, Thomas learned the invaluable lesson that less can indeed be more. By prioritizing quality over quantity in relationships, possessions, and activities, he found the contentment and sense of purpose that had been missing in his previous way of life. He found the feed for his internal need. Thomas's experience underscores that when we choose depth and meaning over superficial abundance, we enrich our lives immeasurably, fostering a sense of satisfaction and well-being that is both profound and lasting.

CULTIVATE DEEP CONNECTIONS

The book highlights the importance of genuine relationships in recovery. It stresses that building a supportive community and fostering deep, meaningful connections can provide the strength and encouragement needed to maintain sobriety and enjoy a richer life. Here are some strategies to help you develop and maintain these vital relationships.

- **Listen Actively:** Genuine listening involves more than just hearing words; it's about understanding the emotions and intentions behind them. Show that you value what the other person is saying through your body language, responses, and attention.

- **Share Openly and Honestly:** Vulnerability fosters deeper connections. Share your thoughts, feelings, and experiences openly with those you trust. This mutual exchange of personal stories and feelings can strengthen bonds.

- **Focus on Fewer, Richer Relationships:** Instead of spreading yourself thin across many superficial relationships, invest more time and energy in nurturing a few relationships that make you feel supported and understood.

- **Make Time:** Consistently set aside time for those important to you. Whether it's a weekly coffee meet-up, a regular phone call, or participating in shared activities, regular engagement keeps relationships strong.

- **Celebrate and Support:** Be there during both the good times and the bad. Celebrate each other's victories and offer support during challenges. This presence in crucial moments can deepen the bond between you.

- **Set Healthy Boundaries:** Understand and communicate your needs and limits in relationships. Healthy boundaries help prevent resentment and misunderstandings, making for more honest and respectful connections.

- **Join Groups That Foster Personal Development:** Participate in groups that align with your recovery goals, such as therapy groups, hobby clubs, or educational classes. These settings provide opportunities to meet like-minded individuals who share similar values and interests.

- **Ask for Honest Feedback:** Sometimes, understanding how others perceive us can help us grow and improve our relational skills. Constructive feedback can guide you in how to be a better friend, partner, or community member.

- **Strive to Understand:** Make a conscious effort to see situations from the other person's perspective. Empathy builds emotional connections and can greatly enhance the quality of your interactions.

By applying these strategies, you can cultivate deeper, more meaningful relationships that will support your recovery journey and enrich every aspect of your life. These connections can become your foundation, offering the love, support, and joy that everyone deserves.

KEEPING THE FAITH.

Faith plays a vital role in the journey of recovery and simplification. It is not just faith in a higher power, but also faith in our own resilience and abilities, and in the support and love of those around us who share in our struggles and triumphs. Each aspect of faith contributes to a holistic recovery process, enabling individuals to navigate the complexities of life with confidence and peace. To truly grasp the transformative power of faith in the recovery process, let us consider the inspiring story of Lisa, whose journey illustrates how deepening faith in various forms can pave the way to lasting recovery and personal fulfillment.

Lisa's story is a testament to the power of faith in the complex journey of recovery. When she first embarked on her path to sobriety, Lisa felt overwhelmed by the magnitude of the challenge ahead. The idea of a life without her dependencies seemed as daunting as it was distant. Yet, it was her faith—both in a higher power and in her own resilience—that anchored her through the stormiest times. Before recovery, Lisa's life was a series of high-stress situations and quick fixes. She often felt adrift, susceptible to the currents of her environment. It was during her first recovery meeting that she encountered the concept of surrendering to a higher power, which initially struck her as a way of giving up her own control. However, as she listened to others share their stories of faith and recovery, she began to see this surrender not as a loss of power but as an acceptance of support beyond her own capabilities.

Lisa started to cultivate faith in her own resilience. She reflected on her past, recognizing moments of strength she hadn't acknowledged before. Each small victory on her journey added layers to her growing sense of self-belief. She also learned to lean on the faith and support of her community. Witnessing others in her support group navigate their recoveries with similar struggles gave her a sense of solidarity and strength. She realized that her faith was multifaceted—not just in spiritual terms but also in the belief in the collective strength of those around her.

Her turning point came one evening during a particularly tough day, where the urge to relapse clawed at her resolve. It was then that she chose to reach out to a fellow group member instead of isolating in her struggle. The conversation that followed wasn't just a distraction but a reinforcement of every piece of faith she had been carefully building. Her friend shared her own moments of doubt and how maintaining faith through those times had led to longer periods of sobriety. This interaction was a powerful reminder for Lisa that faith is dynamic—it grows, it wavers, but it also fortifies over time. Her faith in a higher power gave her a foundation of peace, her faith in herself showed her own strength, and her faith in others provided a safety net of unconditional support.

Today, Lisa shares her story in recovery meetings, not only to affirm her own faith but to ignite it in others. She stands as a beacon of hope to those just starting their journey, embodying the message that through faith—in all its forms—recovery isn't just possible; it's a gateway to a new life filled with confidence, peace, and profound personal growth.

HOLISTIC WELLNESS

Real wellness is about balance. It's about nourishing the body, calming the mind, and enriching the spirit. In recovery, embracing a holistic approach to wellness, incorporating healthy eating, regular exercise, adequate rest, and mindfulness, can transform mere survival into a vibrant, joyful existence. Here's a simple, practical wellness plan that incorporates healthy eating, regular exercise, adequate rest, and mindfulness to support anyone on their recovery journey.

Nourishing The Body.

- **Balanced Diet:** Start by integrating a balanced diet rich in fruits, vegetables, lean proteins, and whole grains. Plan meals that are colorful and diverse, ensuring you receive a broad range of nutrients to support physical recovery and overall health.

- **Hydration:** Aim to drink at least eight glasses of water a day. Staying hydrated helps maintain energy levels, supports kidney health, and can even help manage cravings.

Calming the mind.

- **Daily Mindfulness or Meditation:** Dedicate at least 10-15 minutes each day to mindfulness or meditation. This practice can help reduce stress, lower anxiety levels, and enhance emotional resilience. Apps like Headspace or Calm can be helpful guides for beginners.

- **Regular Sleep Schedule:** Establish a regular sleep schedule by going to bed and waking up at the same time every day. Aim for 7-9 hours of sleep per night to allow your mind and body to rest and regenerate.

Enriching The Spirit.

- **Daily Reflection:** Spend time each day in reflection, whether through journaling, prayer, or quiet contemplation. This practice helps connect with your inner self and align your daily actions with your deeper values.

- **Community Connection:** Engage regularly with a community that supports your recovery. This could be a support group, a religious congregation, or a hobby club where you can share experiences and grow spiritually.

Regular Exercise

- **Structured Physical Activity:** Include at least 30 minutes of moderate exercise into your daily routine. This could be walking, yoga, swimming, or any other physical activity you enjoy. Exercise not only strengthens the body but also boosts mood and helps manage stress.

- **Weekly Flexibility and Strength Training:** Incorporate flexibility exercises like stretching or yoga twice a week, and strength training exercises, such as weightlifting or bodyweight exercises, twice a week to maintain overall body strength and agility.

By following this holistic wellness plan, you're not just surviving; you're actively cultivating a life of balance, health, and joy. Each element of the plan supports the other, leading to a more vibrant and fulfilling existence. Remember, the journey to holistic wellness is gradual, and even small steps can lead to big changes over time.

LIVE WITH PURPOSE

Simplicity isn't about leading a lesser life but about leading a fuller, more purpose-driven life. It's about making room for activities and relationships that truly matter, discarding the rest, and focusing on pursuits that align with personal values and long-term goals. Here are three examples of purpose-driven activities that can help guide you to apply this principle effectively in your own lives.

1. Volunteering

Engage in volunteer work that resonates with your values. Whether it's helping at a local food bank, mentoring youth, or participating in community clean-up events, volunteering provides a sense of purpose and connection to the community. It's an opportunity to give back in a meaningful way while also enriching your own life.

2. Learning and Personal Development

Dedicate time to learning new skills or enhancing existing ones that align with your career goals or personal interests. This could involve taking courses, attending workshops, or simply reading books that expand your knowledge and skills. Continuous learning not only fuels your professional growth but also keeps you mentally sharp and engaged.

3. Mindful Fitness

Incorporate physical activities that not only improve your physical health but also connect with your mental and spiritual goals. Yoga and Tai Chi, for example, offer exercise for the body while also providing space for mental clarity and stress relief.

- **Artistic Expression:** Engage in creative outlets like painting, writing, or playing music. These activities allow you to express your emotions and thoughts in a constructive way, fostering a deep sense of fulfillment and personal identity.

- **Cultivating Relationships:** Actively nurture relationships that are supportive and enriching. Spend quality time with family and friends who understand and share your journey. Prioritizing these relationships can lead to a deeper sense of belonging and joy.

- **Mindful Consumption:** Choose to consume media and products that are beneficial or uplifting. This can mean watching documentaries that inspire, listening to music that soothes or energizes, or buying products from companies that align with your ethical beliefs.

By integrating these purpose-driven activities into your daily life, you can live more intentionally and meaningfully. Each activity should reflect not just a passing interest, but a cornerstone in building a life that is rich with purpose and aligned with your core values. This way, simplicity becomes not about having less, but about having more of what truly matters.

EMBRACE THE JOURNEY

The path to simplicity is continuous. We are on the journey of recovery and simplicity for life. It requires ongoing effort, constant reassessment, and the willingness to let go of what no longer serves us. This journey is one of discovery, trying with challenges but also abundant in rewards. As we conclude this exploration of simplicity in recovery, remember that this book is more than a guide—it is an invitation to transform your life. We've journeyed together, uncovering the immense power of simplicity as a beacon guiding us back to the essentials: honesty, mindfulness, and intentional living. Whether you're in recovery or seeking a more meaningful existence, the core message is clear: simplicity is about much more than decluttering our physical spaces—it's about reshaping our entire approach to life. It's about finding beauty in less, strength in quietness, and making choices that resonate deeply with our values.

This journey of recovery often feels daunting, a path filled with the challenge of changing lifelong habits and facing a future free from dependency. Yet, through the principles of "Keep It Simple," we discover the invaluable wisdom of taking life one day at a time. Each day offers a new opportunity to maintain sobriety, make health-supportive choices, and engage in enriching activities. By embracing the simplicity of daily mindfulness, setting clear intentions, and fostering deep connections, we not only support our recovery but also enhance our overall quality of life. We've discussed how routine and gratitude, along with the pursuit of holistic wellness, form the bedrock of a purposeful and joyful existence.

Now, as you set this book down and continue on your path, I encourage you to pause and reflect: **What is one simple change you can implement today to move towards a more intentional and fulfilling life?** Whether it's setting a daily intention, expressing gratitude for a small joy, or reaching out to forge a supportive connection, choose one action to start your journey towards simplicity. Let this be your call to action: **Start small but start today.** Embrace these principles and integrate them into your daily life. Watch as the transformative power of simplicity reshapes your days, your recovery, and ultimately, your entire existence. In simplicity, we find profound freedom— freedom from addiction, freedom from chaos, and the freedom to live fully and love deeply. Embrace this journey, Keep The Faith, and remember, the simplest approach can often lead to the richest life.

"Keep It Simple," keep it heartfelt, and step forward with confidence and hope into a brighter, simpler tomorrow.

I wish you all well and good fortune on your journey and remember.

"Keep It Simple and Keep The Faith"

APPENDIX 1

Below is a list of contact addresses, phone numbers and websites for a number of Twelve Step and other mutual support programs. **Voices and Faces of Recovery** is a website that maintains a comprehensive listing of all Twelve Step and mutual support organizations.

Website: https://facesandvoicesofrecovery.org/engage/recovery-groups/

Alcoholic Anonymous® AA World Services, Inc.
475 Riverside Drive at West 120th St.11th and 8th Floors New York, NY 10115
Telephone: +1(212) 870 340
Website: https://www.aa.org/

Al-Anon Family Group Headquarters, Inc
1600 Corporate Landing Parkway
Virginia Beach, VA 23454-5617
Telephone: +1 (757) 563 1600
Website: https://al-anon.org/

Narcotics Anonymous
PO Box 9999
Van Nuys_CA 91409
Telephone: +1 (818) 773 9999
Website: https://na.org/

Gamblers Anonymous®
International Service Office
1306 Monte Vista Avenue
Suite 5 Upland, CA 91786

Telephone: +1 (909) 931 9056

Website: https://www.gamblersanonymous.org/

Gam-Anon® Family Group

PO Box 307 Massapequa Park,

NY 11762

Telephone: +1 (718) 352 1671

Website: https://www.gam-anon.org/

All Addicts Anonymous

PO Box 500

Hankins, New York12741

Telephone: +1 (888) 422 2476

Website: https://alladdictsanonymous.org/

APPENDIX 2

I have set out below some books that have had a profoundly positive impact on my Recovery. I hope that they will have the same effect on yours.

- Alcoholics Anonymous (The Big Book) Fourth Edition - Alcoholics Anonymous World Services Inc.
- The Twelve Steps and Twelve Traditions - Alcoholics Anonymous World Services Inc.
- Meditations for the Twelve Step Program - Friends In Recovery
- The Serenity Prayer - Reinhold Niebuhr
- On Becoming A Person – Carl Rodgers
- Emotional Intelligence - Daniel Goleman
- Emotional Agility - Susan David
- Self-Compassion - Kirsten Neff PHD
- Dare to Lead - Brené Brown
- Learned Optimism - Martin E. P. Seligman PHD
- The Worry Trick - David A Carbonell PHD
- Thinking Fast and Slow - Daniel Kahneman
- Awakening Your Power Within - Gerry Hussey
- Mans Search For Meaning - Viktor Frankl
- The Feeling Of What Happens – Antonio Damasio